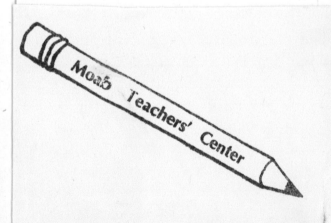

Ray Ginger's JOKEBOOK about AMERICAN HISTORY

Ray Ginger's JOKEBOOK about AMERICAN HISTORY

Compiled and annotated by
RAY GINGER

NEW VIEWPOINTS
A Division of Franklin Watts, Inc.
New York/1974

Library of Congress Cataloging in Publication Data

Ginger, Ray.
  Ray Ginger's jokebook about American history.

  1. American wit and humor. 2. United States—
History—Anecdotes, facetiae, satire, etc. I. Title.
II. Title: Jokebook about American history.
PN6157.G5   973'.02'07   73-22176
ISBN 0-531-05355-5
ISBN 0-531-05562-0 (pbk.)

OTHER BOOKS BY RAY GINGER

Written

The Bending Cross: A Biography of Eugene Victor Debs (1949)

Six Days or Forever?: *Tennessee* v. *John Thomas Scopes* (1958)

Altgeld's America: The Lincoln Ideal versus Changing Realities (1958)

Age of Excess: The United States from 1877 to 1914 (1965)

People on the Move: An Interpretation of American History (1974)

Edited

Spectrum: The World of Science (1959)

American Social Thought (1961)

The Nationalizing of American Life, 1877–1900 (1965)

William Jennings Bryan: Selections (1967)

Modern American Cities (1969)

**FOR
GRANLEY**

vii CONTENTS

The Colonial Period, *1*
City *v.* Country, *13*
Ethnic Jokes, *29*
Regional Jokes, *45*
Class-Conscious Jokes, *77*
Occupational Jokes, *91*
Sex Jokes, *113*
Political Jokes, *121*
Afterword, *137*

FOREWORD

Because of its jocular title, readers might infer that this is not a serious book about the history of the United States. But it is.

In my moments of thinking about the human condition, I have reached two broad distinctions about people that seem workable. One separates those persons who are fundamentally hopeful from those who are basically fearful (the worst fear of all is the dread of making a fool of yourself, the habit of always looking over your shoulder to see what others are thinking of your behavior). Maybe in the future somebody will write a good book about that differentia.

This slight tome, however, springs from my second distinction. Serious folks are not like earnest folks. The latter always have a somber face, much like the couple in Grant Wood's painting "American Gothic." For them, every episode carries some cosmic meaning. In consequence, they miss almost everything important. They are defective in that they do not have much concern for people; they have not learned the lesson preached in Micah, vi:8 ". . . to do justly, and to love mercy, and to walk humbly with thy God?"

Yet abideth these three: faith, hope, and charity, and charity is the noblest of them all. Serious people are charitable people. They are such fools that they care too much about their fellow man. Since their perception of realities is too acute, they frequently fend off the realities by making a joke. As has been said, tragedy tears down the dikes between man and man, while comedy perches on the dikes. But tragedy and comedy have this common virtue: neither of them is earnest. The greatest tragedy, and the greatest comedy, is "King Lear." The United States can offer in reply *Moby Dick* and *The Adventures of Huckleberry Finn.*

These pages contain lesser monuments.

Canmore, Alberta, Canada   RG

Ray Ginger's JOKEBOOK about AMERICAN HISTORY

The Colonial Period

ANECDOTE

One day King Charles I of England asked his court jester to say grace. The jester prayed, "All glory to God on high, and little Laud to the devil." Courtiers chuckled at the slight to Archbishop Laud of the Church of England, who was the chief agent in harassment and prosecution of the dissenting sects.

King: "If the Archbishop hears of this, he'll be after you."
Jester: "I'll hide in a place where he'll never find me."
Charles I: "Where might that be?"
Jester: "In his pulpit, for I'm sure he never goes there."

ITS RELEVANCE

To the minds of dissenters, the Church of England ranked second only to Roman Catholicism in its proximity to the Antichrist. Although sentiments in America often amounted to hatred for Catholics, the more common attitude toward Anglicans was revulsion, or even contempt that verged on indifference. Since the Church of England remained the established church until the Revolution in the Southern colonies, supposedly all residents were members and were required to pay taxes for its support. But law is not always reality. The tax requirement was widely evaded. With the rise of "enthusiastical" creeds such as Methodism in the eighteenth century, they won converts by the thousands away from the cold formalism with its rituals and ceremonies of the Anglican Church.

3   **ANECDOTE**

When enlistments were being taken for King George's War (1744–48; in Europe, the War of the Austrian Succession; in America, it followed the War of Jenkins' Ear), a recruiting sergeant reported to his captain that he had won into their company an extraordinary soldier.

Captain: "Prithee, what is he?"

Sergeant: "A butcher, sir. And we can work him double-time, for we had two sheep thieves already."

ITS RELEVANCE

The techniques of sutlering for European armies have been studied especially by Fritz Redlich, *The German Military Enterpriser and His Work Force* (2 vols., 1964–65). The New World enjoyed more rough-hewn (and probably less legal) devices.

In studying American history it is desirable to use the distinction that would be made at the beginning of the twentieth century by a boss in Tammany Hall: between honest and dishonest graft. Piracy was universally punished by hanging, whereas the legalized piracy called privateering authorized by the government that the ship claimed as "home"—well, that was the wellspring of respectable families in every port in the nation. Similarly with the procurement of supplies on land in wartime. The quartermaster sergeant and his squad might pay for provender with a bill of credit payable years in the future; for an example, see my *People on the Move: An Interpretation of American History* (1974). Or they might simply take the desired goods and cut for the hills.

4 **ANECDOTE**

A British gentleman was riding his horse through the streets of Williamsburg. Coming toward him he saw a young woman, walking, carrying a shoat in her arms. The pig began to scream.

Brit: "My dear, your child cries amazingly."

Woman: "I know it, sir, it always does so when it sees its daddy."

ITS RELEVANCE

Doubtless the resentment of Americans toward resident Britons accelerated in the years after 1763, spurred on by the Stamp Act, the rampant customs officials under the Sugar Act, the ubiquitous presence of regular soldiers, the Intolerable Acts.

But the hostility had always been present. Many Englishmen came to America as royal appointees, securing prestige and profit that colonials selfishly wanted for themselves. Not only was there a conflict of interest between royal governors and general assemblies, but in his contacts with "the common sort" the English gentleman often used the haughty abuse that he had employed against the lower orders at home.

ANECDOTE

A British colonel, Cockburn by name, was reviewing his colonial enlistments. Exceedingly concerned himself with neatness and punctilio, he confronted a private who was extremely dirty.

Cockburn: "How dare you appear on the parade ground in such a dirty shirt? Did you ever see me wear such a filthy garment?"

Soldier: "No, your honor, I never did. But then I took into account that your mistress is a washerwoman."

ITS RELEVANCE

This yarn captures two intense American prejudices: against British, and against officers. Studied insults of this type became more frequent as colonial contacts with English troops were increased.

Until 1763 the colonies relied on militia companies for emergencies such as Indian raids or for their own periodic forays into New France or Florida. But even before British regular soldiers were posted in America, officials in London repeatedly tried to impose English officers on colonial militia companies. This practice was deeply resented by common soldiers—and perhaps even more by American gentlemen who aspired to be officers themselves.

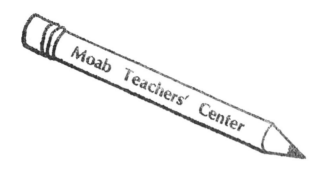

ANECDOTE

"The Father caught the young Fellow naked in Bed with his Daughter. The old Man between Grief and Rage broke out into Reproaches. —You Wretch what do you mean by trying to get my Daughter with Child? The young Fellow answered him, I try to get your Daughter with Child! *I was trying not to get her with Child.*"

ITS RELEVANCE

This tale was told to John Adams while he was practicing law on a circuit that ran as far west as Worcester, and he entered it in his diary under the date of 25 April 1771. The italics are his. Thus did the Founding Fathers spend some of their time, when they were not practicing law, scheming revolution, or farming. Other entries in his diary make clear that Adams knew at second-hand about "the Clap"; see 1759, when he was twenty-three years old; see further Adams to Thomas Jefferson, 9 October 1787 in Lester J. Cappon's splendid edition of *The Adams-Jefferson Letters* (1959).

But Adams also affirmed that he had led a pure life, and most assuredly he should be taken at his word. Another letter to Jefferson (15 November 1813) ends as follows:

"As I have no Amanuenses but females, and there is so much about generation in this letter that I dare not ask any of them to copy it, and as I cannot copy it myself I must beg of you to return it to me. . . ."

ANECDOTE

About 1773 some boys in Boston were playing at enlisting as soldiers. They gathered in the street and went through the routine of calling for volunteers, paying out bounty money, marching away with a flourish, the whole rigmarole as best they understood it. A crowd collected, including some British officers. One boy who presented himself as a volunteer was a sorry specimen—bowlegged, scrawny, ill-coordinated. The sergeant rejected him for service. As he slunk away another lad shouted to the sergeant:

"Call him back, call him back, he'll do for an officer."

ITS RELEVANCE

Once again, contempt for authority. Militia companies had been accustomed to electing their own leaders, and they did not want to have English martinets set up over their heads. Like father, like son; boys took on by osmosis the attitudes of their fathers. Doubtless there was some deliberate indoctrination in anti-British attitudes as 1775 approached, but probably the most effective variety was the automatic and unconscious type.

ANECDOTE

Matters of protocol and precedence ranked very high in the colonial preoccupations. A lawyer and a doctor got into an argument over who should march in front of the other in a ceremonial parade. Unable to agree, they put the problem to the wisest and most judicious elder in town. He pondered the matter, then said: "Let the thief go first, and the executioner walk behind."

ITS RELEVANCE

A paradox: Although Americans have a powerful tendency to vote lawyers into public office, a tendency that has persisted since the origins of the United States, they have never trusted them. Certainly with few exceptions the lawyers of the pre-Revolutionary era were a shabby lot: hardly trained at all, possessing a modicum of law books.

To apply the epithet "executioner" to a physician of the colonial era is doubtless apt. Indeed, as far ahead as the late nineteenth century, we can make a strong brief for Mary Baker Eddy's Christian Science on the simple ground that a doctor was likely to do more harm than good. Only in the twentieth century with the application of statistics to the testing of such preventatives as vaccination for smallpox could medical practice legitimately claim to be a science.

Readers today, accustomed to the vainglory of physicians with their insistence on being called "Dr." (a claim that others with equal right would be embarrassed to assert; who else but an M.D. posts his diploma in his office?), may be startled to hear of the status of doctors at the time of the American Revolution. Of all the "learned professions"—minister, lawyer, civic official, the few college professors—the barber-butcher-executioner-doctor ranked at the foot of the list.

9   **ANECDOTE**

A Scot-American lawyer in New York City was discussing the efficacies of various kinds of poison with General Sir William Howe. They came to the relative merits of laurel versus ratsbane.

General: "We say in England that ratsbane will not kill a lawyer."

Lawyer: "And we say in Scotland that generals are safe from laurel."

ITS RELEVANCE

More studied insults. Marginally it should be noted that Howe, as English generals in America went, was quite competent and was popular in the New World until the conflict came to blows.

Ratsbane—rat poison, particularly trioxide of arsenic.

A lethal dose can be brewed from the broad leaf of some species of laurel.

ANECDOTE

The Battle of Saratoga was quickly followed by the Franco-American Treaty of Amity and Commerce (1778). A few months later, the French ambassador to the Hague encountered the English ambassador.

English ambassador: "You have been guilty of a dishonorable act—no less than that of debauching our daughter."

French ambassador: "I am sorry that you should feel so strongly about it, since she made the first advances, and absolutely threw herself into our arms. But rather than lose your friendship, we are willing to play the honorable part, and marry her."

ITS RELEVANCE

So far as I know, historians agree that the French alliance was highly significant—perhaps crucial to the success of the American Rebellion. This relation holds true from the early loans and supplies of war matériel to the support of a fleet commanded by Admiral Comte de Grasse during the climactic Yorktown campaign.

Felix Gilbert has analyzed the triumphantly small price that the shrewd Americans paid for French support in his *The Beginnings of American Foreign Policy: To the Farewell Address* (paperback 1965), Ch. III. Perhaps the explanation for this scintillating diplomatic victory by the infant United States can be found in the contention of other eminent students: that the Americans' War for Independence was little more than a footnote in the worldwide struggle for empire between England and France. But I find the latter view to be grossly exaggerated.

11   ANECDOTE

A farmer, chancing to be in town, met his parson in a narrow lane. The farmer did not squeeze aside to grant preference as quickly as the minister thought proper.

Parson: "You are better fed than taught."

Farmer: "Very true, for you teach me, and I feed myself."

ITS RELEVANCE

This is an apt tale on the erosion of the "deferential society." It did not collapse; indeed in some ways it still exists in the late years of the twentieth century. But its rougher edges got bevelled down a good bit. Adherents to the older ways, such as George Washington, were flabbergasted when "the common sort" began to assail them verbally after the War for Independence.

The meaning of a deferential society can be found in the memoirs of a Virginian who grew up to be a minister in the Church of England, as deferential a denomination as any Protestant sect to be found in America. He reported that he, as a boy, had hidden in the bushes whenever he found himself approaching a gentleman; the periwig was a sign of an altogether different order of humanity.

ANECDOTE

"So, Susan, my dear," the letter began,
"You've fallen in love with an Englishman.
"Well, they are a manly attractive lot,
"And you happen to like them—which I do not,
"Because I am a Yankee through and through,
"And I don't like them nor the things they do,
" . . ."

ITS RELEVANCE

This fragment of quasi-doggerel was recalled from his adolescence by a colleague (reared in Canada, incidentally). It can almost be counted as an anecdote from the colonial or Revolutionary period since the psychology it expresses springs from the period when the United States was still subservient to the United Kingdom.

Efforts to date to trace down the author (authoress?) have not succeeded. The tone seems appropriate to *Godey's Lady's Book,* a highly successful magazine that lasted for fifty years. But the first issue of its direct predecessor did not appear until 1828.

My instinct tells me to date the poem soon after the War of 1812. Although the War for Independence established the United States as a political entity, it was the economic strength acquired during the Napoleonic Wars that stabilized the new nation and ensured its survival.

City
v.
Country

PLACE NAMES AND SOBRIQUETS

Urban places are fond of grandiloquent names. They call themselves Athens or Syracuse or Ithaca and even Rome. As the locations of these conglomerations suggest, New York and Ohio, this craze was rampant in the early nineteenth century during the Greek and Roman Revivals.

But cities tend to pick up derogatory nicknames: Chicago becomes the Windy City, Pittsburgh the Smoky City. Kansas took the sunflower as its state emblem. A neighboring state officially noted that the sunflower was "a noxious weed." Learning that the offending neighbor had the Eastern goldfinch as its state emblem, the Kansas legislature declared the forementioned feathered creature to be a "common pest."

THEIR RELEVANCE

In spite of the horseplay, place names tend to be drab in the United States. Virginia is a dreary succession of Jonesvilles and Johnsonburgs and Histontowns. Exceptions can be had—Roaring Gap, North Carolina—yet the rule will hold.

Place names seem much more colorful in Canada. Why? Southern Alberta has its Whiskey Gap. Elsewhere in the province you can find Royalties (in the oil fields), Loyalist and Veteran (adjacent towns). When the railroad bypassed a tiny settlement by two miles, the people moved themselves those two miles, and restyled themselves as Champion. Southern Alberta also has a Foremost. Saskatchewan is richer yet. It has Eye Brow. Also Swift Current ("How do you tell Swift Current?" "That's the place with a dog asleep on Main Street.")

Best of all is Newfoundland, with its repertory of names bestowed by itinerant fishermen since the sixteenth century. Within a few miles of St. John's you can visit Cuckold Cove, Cuckold Head, and the town of Dildo.

15   ANECDOTE

A new hand was hired by a Vermont farmer right at the beginning of apple-picking time. The farmer, true to his New England, was both apprehensive and suspicious, since the employee was a total stranger who had just come wandering down the road seeking work. But when the farmer went out to the orchard at noontime, he was amazed. The hand had done a good day's work just in the morning. The two men went into the house for a hearty dinner; then the relieved and grateful farmer helped lug the shiny apples into a shed where there were three barrels.

Farmer (pointing): "Perfect ones in here. Bruised ones in there; we use them for cider and applejack. Wormy ones over yonder, and I pray to God that barrel stays empty." The farmer went away. When he went back at supper time, all three of the barrels were empty. Every basket was still full. Not one apple had been sorted. The new hand was lying comfortably on his back in the middle of the shed.

Farmer: "What in the name of God's the matter with you, man?"

Hand: "Jes' cain't face these decisions."

ITS RELEVANCE

Everybody will know the character type, which does not belong exclusively to farmhands. When the late John Maurice Clark of Columbia told me this yarn, he was talking about the dilemmas that face a writer.

But toilers in New England agriculture, for more than a century, have had special reasons for lacking initiative. One family in Dorset, Vermont is still on land that their family has occupied since before 1800. The current residents work the apple orchards. But they no longer own them. Title is now held by a Texas oil man.

ANECDOTE

A farm hand painfully accumulated enough cash to buy a little land of his own. Then he worked for years to improve it. He cleared more acres. He planted a greater variety of crops. He patched the roof on the shanty. He even splashed around some paint.

When the property was in pretty fair shape, the minister came by on one of his pastoral calls. The owner proudly conducted the clergyman around the grounds. The cleric, impressed, said solemnly, "God and Thee have a right nice little farm here."

"Yeah? You should have seen the place when God was running it on his own."

ITS RELEVANCE

The wilderness quickly invades a deserted property and reclaims its own. This phenomenon can happen even to a still occupied piece of land, as Ellen Glasgow depicted so brilliantly with her symbol in *Barren Ground* (1925) of the encroaching broomsedge. But the process was accelerated in the United States because the mobility of the rural population—like the mobility of most other folks—has been so high. It was all too common for a family to partially clear a patch, work it for a few years, and then saunter on westward. As late as 1905, half of all farmers in the United States were tilling tracts where they had not been located at the dawn of the century.

Anybody crossing the country by car can see, in all regions, the abandoned farmhouses. Many of these are the product of the consolidation of several holdings into one; others have resulted from the decision of a prospering owner to move his family into a new house in town, and commute. But frequently the area once under cultivation has been abandoned also.

ANECDOTE

A farmer in mid-Dakota in 1877 had an utterly miserable year.

Item: Spring was unusually wet so he was late getting his wheat planted.

Item: Drought hit in the summer.

Item: For the third straight year, a plague of locusts struck. Not only did they eat the crops, they ate feather blankets off the beds. They even gnawed on the plowhandles.

Item: One day the farmer's wife saw him standing in a field shaking his fist at the sky and bellowing:

"Goddam the Great Northern Railroad."

ITS RELEVANCE

Plainly the man had been frustrated to the verge of dementia. But the grievances of farmers against railroads were clear enough. To look at only one example, we might take the long-haul short-haul complaint. East of the Mississippi River, a railroad at nearly every point on its line had to meet competition, not only from other railways but perhaps also from water transportation on rivers or on the Erie Canal. But west of the Mississippi, a railroad often had a monopoly over an extended stretch of track. It might cost more to ship a given lot of freight from mid-Dakota to San Francisco than to ship the same goods from Chicago to the Bay.

In spite of the above story, the Great Northern was the most efficient and (to farmers) the most helpful company in this vast region. Its president James J. Hill had a deliberate policy of aiding farmers in the improvement of their operations; he helped, for instance, to import more suitable breeds of cattle. Obviously his motives were not unselfish, but he did not deserve to be blamed for all the afflictions of the Great Plains.

A Blackfoot chief in Montana in 1897 wanted to go to Washington to urge the treaty rights of his band, but he did not have the cash to buy a railroad ticket. Another, more worldly, chief told him that he could borrow from a bank in Great Falls. He went there and was referred to the cashier. He finally communicated his request to borrow $500.

Cashier: "What can you put up for collateral?"

Chief: "What that?"

Cashier: "What do you own that would give us some security on our loan?"

Chief: "Own maybe 3,000 horses."

Cashier: "Please come back in three days and we'll give you an answer."

An investigator was sent by the bank. He snooped around, and reported that common opinion had the chief as owning at least 3,000 horses. Papers were waiting for the chief when he came back to Great Falls. He signed and held out his hand for the money.

Cashier: "Chief, it might be dangerous to carry all that money around. Why don't you just leave it here—it's called a demand deposit—and we'll honor any check you write until the total reaches $500."

Chief: "Hunh, how many horses you own?"

ITS RELEVANCE

Banks depend on tradition: they can function only when people trust them. Without the general confidence, a banking system cannot expand and contract the supply of credit; that is, of money. Sound banks run on faith, others run on the Grace of God.

ANECDOTE

A wheat farmer in South Dakota in 1935 won $126,000 in the Irish Sweepstakes. No such sum of money had been heard of in the state for years, so a newspaper sent a reporter to ask the recipient what he planned to do with his windfall. "Well," he said, "I been farming for so long—and I just love farming—that I reckon I'll go on farming 'till the money runs out."

ITS RELEVANCE

Not far behind this whimsical yarn is an abysmal truth. The price of a bushel of wheat in 1935 was $.83, whereas in 1919 it had been $2.16. On the other side, farmers were still meeting their monthly payments on mortgages, contracted in more buoyant times to buy more equipment, at the same number of dollars per month prescribed in the original contract even though the value of the dollar had gone up by double. Farmers were burning corn in their stoves to heat the house and to cook meals; they were dumping milk cans onto the roads to keep milk off the market so that prices would rise.

ANECDOTE

A mountaineer from Kentucky had despaired of wringing any sort of livelihood from his patch of land, and had migrated to Chicago. He was beaten there too, until he concluded that he'd might as well go home to die among his kinfolk. Going to see a carpenter, he said he needed a box 2" x 2" x 40'. The carpenter opined as how he could make it, but why. "Gotta ship my clothesline home."

ITS RELEVANCE

The notion that all hillbillies are insufferably stupid is just another stereotype, as misleading and libelous as the others.

But the assertion that many hillbillies have wanted to come down from the mountains to the city is a major historical truth.

"How can you get ten rednecks into a VW Beetle?"

"I dunno."

"Tell them you're going to St. Louis."

ANECDOTE

A migrant from West Virginia was standing on a manhole cover in the middle of the street at the corner of Roosevelt Road and State Street in Chicago. Every thirty seconds he jumped into the air, clapped his hands, and shouted "26." Such aberrant behavior would attract a crowd anywhere. Folks gathered and laughed. The foreigner said nothing, just went ahead with his business. At length, one man, bolder than the others, stepped out and said "Hey rube, that looks like fun. Mind if I try?" Not changing his expression, the West Virginian moved off the manhole and gestured the native onto it.

The Chicagoan jumped into the air and started to clap his hands. Quicker than a lizard's tongue, the migrant snatched away the cover and the Chicagoan fell into the sewer. The West Virginian solemnly replaced the lid, stepped onto it, jumped in the air, clapped his hands, and shouted "27."

ITS RELEVANCE

Animosities between regions have often been intense in the United States. One common example is "town versus gown," where the aborigines surrounding a university feel intense resentment of its apparent idleness and wealth. Adolescents in Cambridge love to beat on a Harvard student, especially if he is wearing a tuxedo. Gangs in Waltham used to wander through the parking lots to break off the radio aerials and windshield wipers.

These roles can be reversed in jokes, so that the migrant to a big city gets his revenge against the locals who have tormented him. Man bites dog.

ANECDOTE

This lil ol' country boy from North Carolina had been doing so well in stock-car races and on the dirt tracks that he got offered a car for the 500-mile race at Indianapolis. While he was burning up the bricks in his trial runs and then in the qualifying tests, the chief of his pit crew was explaining to him the rules of the race. One specified that each driver had to make at least three stops to refuel.

After the race the pit chief was seen in a bar in Indianapolis, where he was heard to remark: "That damn redneck fool should have won, but he blew $160,000 for all of us. He made his three stops for gas all right, but he also made five to ask for directions."

ITS RELEVANCE

Whether a person cares especially about automobile racing or not is irrelevant. The Indy 500 must be one of the greatest public spectaculars. As with Epsom Downs, you should go at least once. A crowd of 300,000 is bound to contain some weird customers. While cars were roaring past at 200 miles per hour not fifty feet away, a small boy patiently worked at building his own tower of Pepsi Cola cans. When they release 10,000 balloons into the sunny azure before the race begins, it is something beautiful.

A man who drives regularly in sports-car races speaks contemptuously of the Indianapolis event as a test of equipment, not of drivers. All you need to know, he says, is "Turn left, Turn left."

ANECDOTES

One town in northern Mississippi is so far back in the piney woods they have to pipe in sunlight.

The same principality is so tiny they built the town hall on top of the Dairy Queen.

William Faulkner, a native of Oxford in the same part of the state, explained why you should run a whorehouse behind your ice-cream parlor: you never use up the merchandise, and the depreciation is mighty low.

A village in North Carolina is so hick that the general store keeps the Velveeta on the Gourmet Foods shelf.

THEIR RELEVANCE

Perhaps no Americans knew their country better than the performers in circuses, operas, and touring dramatic companies. Do you remember Minnie Maddern Fiske, from real life, or the Duke and Dauphin from *The Adventures of Huckleberry Finn?* The touring artists struck out at their patrons in small towns:

"Hey, rube, wanna mixt it."

"I'll fight you until Hell freezes over, and then I'll scratch on the ice, 'C'mon, you bastards.' "

M. Lemieux owned nearly half of Bienville Parish in Louisiana and the McDade family held most of the rest. They both had children of marriageable age, and patriarch McDade got the notion that if the two clans would merge they could form a true dynasty. He urged his son Willie Jack to start courting Charlotte Lemieux. The resultant liaison went on for some weeks, until a sheepish Willie Jack appeared before his father.

Lad: "Shucks, dad, I can't marry her. She's a virgin."

Father: "That's right, son, ain't good enough for her own folk, ain't good enough for us."

ITS RELEVANCE

Although considerable evidence exists on the topic of sexual intercourse between white masters and black slaves ("superordinate" and "subordinate" as some sociologists would say—ugh), we will never have good statistics on the frequency of incest. But the paucity of evidence does not eliminate the possibility of a gibe.

In the ongoing clash of townsman against cosmopolite, each group has accused the other of being sexually loose. Everybody has heard dozens of dirty jokes about the farmer's daughter. As for those wild parties in New York—well!

And yet, we might wonder if these fantasies have not broken beyond their boundaries. I have heard about the lewdness of farmer's daughters from farmers, and about the degeneracy of urban top-hats from urban top-hats. Perhaps sexual fantasy knows no limits.

25   ANECDOTE

A nubile girl on a Vermont farm, far from being the brightest lass in the county, became aware at last that she was pregnant. She had to tell her father, who still had not realized the fact because he was no more perceptive than his daughter. He pondered the matter.

Father: "Daughter, who was the feller that knocked you up."

She: "Daddy, when you bin hit by a buzz saw, how do you tell which tooth cut?"

ITS RELEVANCE

This one came from Shepherd B. Clough of Columbia University, who used it to deride all monocausal theories of economic history.

ANECDOTE

A Vermont farmer turned up at the blacksmith's with a broken wheel from his wagon. Like any jack-of-all-trades, he had fixed the wooden rim himself, but he needed a metal flange. The blacksmith went to work on the job. Between blows with his hammer, he questioned.

Blacksmith: "Who broke it?" Tap, tap, tap

Farmer: "Hired man." Tap, tap, tap

Blacksmith: "How'd 'e do thet?"

Farmer: "Druv it in a hole." Tap, tap, tap

Blacksmith: "Same hired man ruint your daughter?" Tap, tap, tap

Farmer: "Yep." Tap, tap, tap

Blacksmith: "Keerless chap, hain't 'e."

ITS RELEVANCE

The signature, so to speak, of natives of northern New England is that they are men of few words. To use their characteristic understatement, they are laconic.

ANECDOTE

Conversation overheard in a small town in Maine:
First Man: "Djuh hear Bob Small got arrested?"
Second Man: "What was he doing?"
First Man: "Overthrowing the government."

ITS RELEVANCE

The outlanders have their own ways of spoofing the metropolis. Each of these men was lying, and each knew that the other was lying. What we have is a folksy, but brilliant, example of "perspective by incongruity." During that incredible period from 1947 to 1960 (which might properly be called the Truman Era or the Nixon Era but for which the label "McCarthy Years" is far-fetched) when most of the nation was insane with fears of plots to overthrow the government, these two Down Easters were chortling at the absurdity of it and congratulating themselves that they were aloof from the madness. They knew that Bob Small might get drunk sometimes, but he wasn't going to do any permanent damage.

Besides, there wasn't any government around here worth overthrowing.

28   **ANECDOTE**

One tiny farming village in New Hampshire has a Volunteer Fire Department. The building does not contain a telephone.

ITS RELEVANCE

For generations an honored tradition in the United States was that certain places and occupations were for men, others for women. Only after supper did the two sexes mingle much. And the men in this Volunteer Fire Company definitely do not want them to mingle on Saturday afternoon, when the men gather at the Station for the weekly pinochle game. With them, the game is played in deadly earnest. Nobody wants to be bothered by the little woman phoning with a shopping list. In comparison, destruction of a house by fire is a picayune concern.

These volunteer fire companies can be paralleled on a much higher social level by the exclusive men's clubs of big cities: the Harvard or the Cosmopolitan in New York, the Union League in Chicago, the Somerset in Boston, the Racquet Club in Philadelphia. In the United States such clubs are drying up and dying out under the pressures of increased costs combined with a shortage of skilled help. Out of fiscal desperation, nearly all now admit women. Abroad, however, the exclusive club may be gaining in prestige. It is reported that ambitious but socially undesirable young men have sought admission to membership on their promise never to come near the place.

Ethnic Jokes

Each of four Scots, while swimming, bet a dollar that he could stay under water longer than any of his fellows. All drowned.

Q. "Why are you late to work, Macmullen?"

A. "Squeezed the toothpaste tube and got too much. Took me an hour to put it back."

An advertisement for a funeral parlor in Camden, South Carolina stated: "Bargains in coffins." Fourteen suicides occurred that day.

A Scottish child killed his parents so that he could go free to the annual picnic of the Orphans' Society.

"Did ye hear about Ramsay? Scalped by the Indians. Poor chap. Just two days since he paid fifty cents for a haircut."

THEIR RELEVANCE

Virtually without exception, jokes against the Scots in America have focussed on one charge: They are covetous. A few hours reading in the business correspondence of Scottish and Scot-Irish merchants and cotton factors of the eighteenth century might make anybody wonder if this canard did not originate from hard realities.

Persons not American are referred to the practices, mid-twentieth century, of Scottish bankers on Bay Street in Toronto or Sherbrooke Street in Montreal.

ANECDOTE

"Why is the wheelbarrow the greatest invention ever made?"

"It taught a few Irishmen to walk on their hind legs."

ITS RELEVANCE

Slurs against the Irish-Americans have assuredly not disappeared. But their greatest incidence was probably in the years around 1850, when the massive incidence of immigrants from Eire took place. The figures for immigrants from Ireland read thusly (in hundreds of thousands):

1846	.51
1847	1.06
1848	1.13
1849	1.59
1850	1.64
1851	2.21

Since the total population of the United States at this time was hovering around 25 million, so huge an influx of an alien group was certain to create tensions. Many home-grown Americans did not care a whit that the Irish peasant was fleeing from successive crop failures which could and did mean starvation for the masses in Ireland. Nor was an American comforted by noting that the newcomers were Catholic, and that many of them were not literate in any language. Some consequences of this culture conflict are revealed on the next page.

ANECDOTE

An Irish GFU living in Brooklyn could never do anything right. When he tried to lift a hundred pound bag of grain on the docks he dropped it on his foot. When he got married, his wife soon proved to be a drunkard. His luck was consistently bad until he got that letter from a firm of solicitors in Sydney. An uncle had left him £1,000 in his will. If he would present himself at the firm's offices with proof of his identity, the bequest could be paid at once. He did not have the air fare to Australia, but Travellers' Aid managed to raise it for him as a loan.

When he got to Sydney, he was told that a clerical error had been made; he was not entitled to any inheritance at all. Tearfully he boarded the plane to return to his dreary job in Brooklyn—in debt to Travellers' Aid. Fifty miles off the coast of Australia the right front engine on the jet cut off. Using a stewardess as an intermediary he got in to see the pilot, to whom he explained that he was a jinx, with him on board, everybody would die. He wanted a parachute to bail out. The pilot said No; then his left front engine went dead. So reluctantly he agreed.

The nebbish jumped through the escape hatch. His chute wouldn't open. As he hurtled through the clouds he prayed:

"St. Francis, St. Francis, be with me now."

A gigantic fist came out of the clouds and clutched his collar to bring him to a teeth-jarring stop: "St. Francis Xavier or St. Francis Assisi?"

"St. Francis Assisi."

The fist opened.

ITS RELEVANCE

Italian-Americans have always resented Irish and German domination of the Church in the United States. If you are Irish, do not pray to the patron saint of Italy.

ANECDOTE

Pat and Mike were ambling along a railroad track. As they saw a train approaching, they slanted off the right of way. Just then a bull came charging past straight at the locomotive. The cow-catcher caught him and knocked him horns over heels right back into the pasture. Pat scratched his head and mused:

"Sure, I admire his courage, but I deplore his discretion."

ITS RELEVANCE

In 1966 both seats from Virginia in the Senate of the United States were vacant. A contractor in Hampton, black and holding considerable sway in his community, was invited to talk about Southern politics to a group of high-school students drawn from all over the nation. When he stated that he was supporting the nominees of the Byrd machine for both Senate seats, some members of the audience could not believe what they had heard.

In reply, the contractor told this same story. His version involved a rabbit and a monkey. The key words in the punch line were "nerve" and "judgment."

Some of the students still looked as if they had met Machiavelli (not a bad guy either, for that matter). As we left the classroom, one student remarked: "Isn't it remarkable that American politics can accommodate a man like that?" Another teacher replied: "You idiot, American politics *is* men like that."

ANECDOTE

Along about 1897 a man left his exclusively Norwegian-American farming community in Minnesota. It was early spring, roads were still covered with snow interspersed with patches of ice, and he was driving a sleigh pulled by a horse. Just as he rounded a bend a human figure lurched out of the woods directly in front of him. He tried to turn, but the sleigh skidded and hit the man an awful blow, knocking him into a tree. He suffered a skull fracture and a broken neck. When the driver Mr. Lie reached the victim, he was dead.

Lie sorrowfully loaded the corpse into the sleigh and headed for the nearest town, where he sought out the constable. He explained how the accident had happened, and where.

Constable Bakken: Well, let's have a look at the body."
They did so. "Ah, it's just Johannsen, that dumb Swede."

Lie began again to assert his innocence.

Constable Bakken: "Aw, forget it. But you'll have to go to the county seat to collect your bounty."

ITS RELEVANCE

Bounties have been paid in American history by governments that sought to promote a good (English bounties on indigo in the eighteenth century) or to eradicate an evil (payments for every dead wolf or other predator). This tale gives an original meaning to a recurrent form of government action.

Animosity between Norwegian-Americans and Swedish-Americans was exasperated by World War II, when Norway underwent Nazi occupation for five years while Sweden remained neutral.

Question and Answer

"How do you tell the bride at a Polish wedding?"

"She's the one with the braided armpits."

Question and Answer

"How do you tell the bride at a Polish wedding?"

"She's the one in the clean sweatshirt."

Question and Answer

"Where's the best place to hide your money in a Polish household?"

"Under the soap."

Question and Answer

"Why don't they let Polacks swim in Lake Michigan?"

"They leave a ring."

Question and Answer

"How can you identify the Polish Air Force?"

"The planes have hair under the wings."

Question and Answer

"Why is the suicide rate so low among Polacks?"

"How can you kill yourself jumping from a basement window?"

THEIR RELEVANCE

Nobody can doubt the malice that underlies this stereotype. But when a wave of so-called Polack jokes began to sweep the nation about 1965, it quickly became obvious that intelligence of a high level was being expended on inventing them. Many of these jibes were funny without ceasing to be cruel and unjustified. The phenomenon of brains spent on vindictiveness is not easy to explain. My hunch is that Irish-Americans in Chicago thought the Polish-Americans were getting too many jobs on the city payroll.

Question and Answer

"How many Polacks does it take to change a light bulb?"

"Three. One to hold the bulb and two to turn the ladder."

Question and Answer

"What do they do with stupid Italians?"

"Send them to Poland to be university presidents."

Two Polacks were trying to hang a picture:

First Polack: (holding head of nail against the wall and banging on the point with a hammer). "It won't go in."

Second Polack: "You dummy, that nail's for the other wall."

Two Polacks were fishing in a rowboat:

First Polack: "I'm hungry. Let's go get something to eat."

Second Polack: "But this is a great spot. The fish are really biting."

First Polack: "I'll fix it so we can find it again." He took out a pencil and marked an X on the floor of the boat.

THEIR RELEVANCE

Slander against Polish people has turned relentlessly on two themes. Examples of one refrain are given on the preceding page: "Polacks are filthy" (almost animals in fact; they even live underground like troglodytes). Above is the other canard: "Polacks are stupid."

ANECDOTES

Question and Answer

"How does a Polack tighten his clothesline?"

"He moves his house back four feet."

Question and Answer

"Why are there only two pallbearers at a Polish funeral?"

"That's all you need to carry a garbage can."

THEIR RELEVANCE

This duet can serve as the closing medley of Polack jokes:
"They are stupid." "They are filthy."

Question and Answer

"How does the Italian army train for World War III?"

Answer: Raise both hands above your head.

The typical Italian male in the Piedmont or the Aosta Valley enters a church only three times, and every time he must be carried in: to his baptism, to his wedding, and to his funeral.

Question and Answer

"You don't think an Italian is a white man, do you?"

"No sir, he is a dago."

Question and Answer

"How did God create Italians?"

"Well, he reached down with one hand and he swooped up a handful of mud, and he reached down with the other hand and scooped up a handful of grease, and he smacked his hands together, and they went: WOP."

THEIR RELEVANCE

We could make a hate-spectrum for the ordinary white Anglo-Saxon Protestants in the United States. Until about 1950, I would have been sure that American blacks evoked the worst hostility. But by the time I left New York in 1960, recent immigrants from Puerto Rico seemed to be arousing even more antagonism than did native-born Negroes. However these details of interpretation may be adjusted, I feel no doubt that the chief single factor in stimulating hatred is skin-color.

This phenomenon, which in itself almost stupefies me, is rendered even more puzzling when Italians are tarnished by it. Although a Sicilian is likely to have a dark skin, a Piedmontese might well have a fair skin and blond hair. But the latter are not featured in films about the Mafia.

ANECDOTE

A Jewish bachelor, age 38, had at last managed to move out of the apartment of his widowed mother. But every Friday evening he made his obligatory pilgrimage to Grand Concourse in the Bronx, knowing that he would have gefilte fish and chicken soup with matzo balls. Shortly after Chanukkah one winter he trudged from the subway through the snow to his mother's home. She hurried into the foyer to meet him, even helping him to take his overcoat off. When he removed his scarf, she shot a glance at his necktie, a new present from her, and said

"Ah, Joey, didn't you like the other one?"

ITS RELEVANCE

American wave lengths tingle with anti-Semitic stories. The "Jewish mother" joke is a comparatively mild form, and of all the ones that I have heard, this seems to me to be one of the funniest.

Anti-mother yarns are not limited to the Jewish community. One mother, pure WASP, never thought that any of her five children was sufficiently grateful. She also knew that they never did anything right.

One son: "That woman would have had several helpful suggestions if she had been around at the Creation."

And again: "I never yet put mustard on a sandwich that she didn't think tomato catsup would have been better."

ANECDOTE

A Jewish recruit from Brooklyn, at the very beginning of his basic training, turned up religiously every morning on sick call. Doctors treated him peremptorily, gave him the traditional two aspirins, and sent him back to duty. At last came the morning when he encountered a Jewish doctor, also from Brooklyn, who examined him thoroughly, and then asked where he hurt.

"My chest. Right here."

"How does it hurt?"

"I used to have feelings there that I don't have any more."

"Look, Mac, you don't *have* to have heartburn to be healthy."

ITS RELEVANCE

Of all the ethnic cuisines that I have eaten, Jewish is the worst. My first insight into this bewilderment came soon after World War II in Ann Arbor, Michigan, when the local chapter of Hadassah brought out *Like Mama Used to Make: A Collection of Favorite and Traditional Jewish Dishes.* Going through this little book of recipes made me realize that the ingredients of the typical dish were the foods that would have been cheap in Russia or Poland seventy-five years ago: barley, potatoes, onions, apples, shortening. Yet here were these affluent women in the United States trying to preserve the hereditary recipes—and giving their families a chronic heartburn. Try eating kasha, with its overload of chicken fat.

41 ANECDOTE

As he marched up the Golden Stairs toward the Pearly Gates, the late Reverend Mr. Lee, a black Baptist pastor from Mississippi, found himself shoulder to shoulder with the late Cardinal of Chicago and a late rabbi of world renown for his scholarly achievements. They reached the top. St. Peter said: "You three gentlemen have all led exemplary lives. No doubt you are entitled to enter here. But we do have one last requirement for entrance. Each of you must ask me a question that I cannot answer." The rabbi posed a conundrum based on a Hebrew text of the Bible. A perfect reply came flying back, and the rabbi wearily trudged off down the Stairs. The Cardinal framed his query, in Latin, around a little known portion of Revelations. Exit the Cardinal. As he left, Mr. Lee followed him.

St. Peter: "Mr. Lee, you haven't asked your question."

Lee: "Your Eminence, it's no use. Those two gentlemen asked you questions where I couldn't even understand the question, and you answered them right back. What chance have I got?"

He walked on down the Stairs.

St. Peter: "Well, nigger, you can at least try!"

Lee: "Well, St. Peter, it won't help me to get in, but there is one problem that's bothered me for a long time, and maybe you can help me with it. When's us black folks gonna get together?"

St. Peter: "Come on in."

ITS RELEVANCE

My son Tom, in 1973 a student in the School of Law at the University of Mississippi, tells me that this joke normally opens a meeting in a Negro church to organize a protest demonstration or some other disruption of white man's order. It is almost as traditional as playing the Star Spangled Banner before an NFL game.

A Negro family moved into Mamaroneck in Westchester County, one of the wealthiest suburbs of New York City. They had a son, age five. It happened that their nearest neighbors, white, also had a five-year-old boy. The two lads quickly developed the habit of meeting on their property lines each morning to exchange insults. First morning:

White boy: "We just came back from two weeks in Bermuda."

Black boy: "We moved in here straight from three weeks at Nassau."

Second morning:

White boy: "We own two Cadillacs and an Olds 98."

Black boy: "We got two GTO's, a Lincoln Continental, plus a Jaguar."

Third morning:

White boy: "We have two downstairs maids and an upstairs maid."

Black boy: "We got all them, and a butler. Besides, we ain't got niggers living next door."

ITS RELEVANCE

The rediscovery of irony is one of the few achievements of the United States in the decade after 1950. Beside this, the ill-named "McCarthy Era" is piddling.

43   ANECDOTE

Soon after the Supreme Court decided *Brown* v. *Board of Education of Topeka* (1954), a plantation owner in the Mississippi Delta swaggered belligerently up to one of his black sharecroppers.

Owner: "How yall feel 'bout the integration business, Mose?"

Mose: "Ah'se neutral, boss. Got plenny relatives both sides."

ITS RELEVANCE

One evening standing in his back yard in Hampton, Virginia, after feeding us a wonderful dinner of fried chicken with corn on the cob, B. N. Puryear (legally black but visually light brown) said: "Nobody can tell me a thing about integration. Look at me. I've been integrated."

When we were asking for directions to his home, he ended: "You can't miss it. Circular driveway. Pick-up and two cars—all white." Maybe the last laugh will be his.

Regional
Jokes

Petaluma, California calls itself "the egg capital of the world." It also is "the hand-wrestling capital of the world," and hosts a championship contest every year.

A town in the northern part of the lower peninsula of Michigan (I can't even remember its name) has posted billboards for hundreds of miles around to proclaim that it has, on the grounds of a Catholic retreat, the largest cross in the world. Could any blasphemy exceed this one?

Tomah, Wisconsin has a sign on its main street to announce that it is "The Home of Frank Smith." When I drive past a huge poster on Route 69 from Sudbury to Toronto which proclaims "Parry Sound is the home of Bobby Orr," I recognize the name. When Mitchell, South Dakota tells me in large letters that it is the home of George McGovern, I know the name. But has anybody outside of Tomah heard of Frank Smith?

THEIR RELEVANCE

Be a booster, not a knocker, as Sinclair Lewis chortled in his *Babbitt* (1922). Transylvania College in Lexington, Kentucky tried to boom itself a hundred and fifty years ago as "the Harvard of the West." Doubtless other schools tried the same tack. Towns were constantly trying to come up with a catchy slogan, hoping that it might help to make them a county seat, a junction point on the railroad.

Many individuals share this penchant for self-advertisement. Clarence Darrow and Lincoln Steffens both published their memoirs within a period of about a year around 1931. Darrow wrote to his old friend Steffens that everybody seemed to be standing around on street corners while pounding on kettle drums and shrieking: Hey, for Pete's sake, look at me for a minute.

ANECDOTE

An oil company with headquarters in Houston determined to build the tallest tower in the world with a revolving restaurant on the top. It was frankly intended to be a self-promotional device. Because of ties across the border, several of the Texas executives had seen a similar structure in Calgary, Alberta named for another oil company—this was the Husky Tower. They wrote to the management of Husky to ask the height of their phallic edifice. Having an answer, they put up their building.

When they had finished it so that it lowered over the skyline of Houston, revolving restaurant and all, they got a registered letter from Calgary: Ha, ha, we lied to you. Our building is twelve feet taller than yours. We're still #1.

ITS RELEVANCE

Many businessmen who regard themselves as adults indulge in this type of juvenilia. Maybe it really is good business. The self-fulfilling prophecy is a common phenomenon in many cultures; as long as nearly everybody believes that prices on the New York Stock Exchange are going to rise, prices on the Big Board will indeed rise.

Gadgets like the Husky Tower are not intended simply to advertise the Husky Oil Company. They are also meant to boost the city. For that purpose, no technique is too shoddy. For instance, a typical resident of Sauk Center, Minnesota fifty years ago would not have told Sinclair Lewis the time of day. A five-dollar bill would not have bought him a cup of coffee. But now the town proclaims itself to be "The Original Main Street."

George Washington, age 9, was born on a large ranch in western Texas, more than two centuries ago. The only shade anywhere around the ranchhouse was a large saguaro cactus which protected the bedroom window. George's father came home one afternoon from the range to find that this favored cactus had been deliberately chopped down. Enraged, he summoned George.

Father: "George, did you cut down my cactus?"

George: "Father, I did it with my little hatchet. I cannot tell a lie."

Father: "Mother, start packing up. George will never make out in Texas."

ITS RELEVANCE

The story about George Washington and the cherry tree has no foundation in fact (seemingly it was invented by Parson Mason Weems for his pamphlet biography of 1800). The yarn above also has no foundation in fact; Were there any Anglos in Texas in 1732, when Washington was born?

What the story reveals is an intense hostility of many twentieth-century Americans toward Texans. Beside the indictment that they are braggarts lies the charge that they are not straightforward. It is recorded that White House correspondents had this to say about Lyndon B. Johnson, the first President from Texas. On Johnson's mannerisms: "When the President smooths down the hair on the back of his head, he's telling the truth; when he strokes the side of his nose, he's telling the truth; when he rubs his hands, he's telling the truth; but when his lips move, he's lying."

ANECDOTE

A Texas oil man had made an important strike; the field promised to yield hundreds of millions of barrels of crude. To celebrate, he ordered a custom-built Lincoln Continental. The day it arrived in Dallas, he immediately drove out to the country club to show off to his buddies. Enlisting several passengers, he ushered them into the limousine and installed himself behind the wheel. Then he took off his eyeglasses and tossed them onto the shelf above the dashboard. There were instant protests. Both rear doors opened.

"Hey, Tom, put those things back on. You're blind as a bat."

"Nevah mind. Win'shields ground to my prescription."

ITS RELEVANCE

Due in considerable measure to the depletion allowance on oil fields that gives the owners a large tax shelter on their investments, oil men, especially in the Southwest, have in the twentieth century been the one sizable group that has flamboyantly advertised its wealth.

Also oil women. One widow with an inheritance in oil frequently went to inspect her holdings near Baton Rouge, Louisiana. She always stayed in the city at the same hotel, where she liked to get the same suite. She thought of it as hers. Came the evening when she arrived only to be told that the suite was already engaged. Acting through agents, she bought the land just across the street from the delinquent hostelry and built her own luxury hotel. It charged $1 per day for rooms until the doomed hotel went bankrupt.

ANECDOTE

Two Texas oil men went to lunch together in Houston. After lunch as they strolled along, their return route took them past the Cadillac agency.

First man: "Let's go in and look around."

Second man: "OK."

Two new models were in the display room, both four-door sedans, one gray and one black.

First man: "Think Ah'll take the black, 'less yuh want it."

Second man: "Nah, got uh black. Ah'll take thuh gray."

They signed the papers and asked to have the cars delivered. The first man reached for his checkbook in his breast pocket.

Second man: "Nah, Ah'll take care of it. You got lunch."

ITS RELEVANCE

The life style that prompts these people to be such roistering spendthrifts deserves much more thoughtful study than it has received. They flaunt not only their wealth but also their uncouth behavior. They show what they are; they simply do not know how to be couth.

I once worked for Henry Holt and Company, one of the oldest and most respectable book publishers in the nation. It had passed under the control of Clint Murchison, now dead but then one of the wealthiest of all Texas millionaires. His personal representative on the board of directors was Don Edwards, who perhaps had never read a single book, but he had been allied with Clint when they brought in some gushers. The secretary to the chairman of the board once observed wryly:

"You can always tell when the directors are meeting. You keep seeing Mr. Edwards' Clark Bar wrappers all over the carpet."

ANECDOTE

Three Texans, identifying each other by their booming voices and their distinctive accent, were drinking together at the Men's Bar in the Biltmore adjacent to Grand Central Station in New York. Although they had never met before, one began soon to boast about his property.

First man: "Ah own 15,000 acres, 2,300 head of cattle, and eleven oil wells."

Second man: "Ah only own 11,000 acres and 2,100 head, but Ah got nineteen oil wells."

Third man: "Ah own twenty acres" (Others guffaw) "—in downtown Houston."

ITS RELEVANCE

This jibe at Texas braggadocio contains a profound truth about American history. If we divide the economy into broad sectors, probably more profit has been made in real estate than in any other sphere of the economy: more than in manufacturing, or banking, or insurance, certainly more than in transportation. One thinks of Marshall Field in terms of his famous department store, but the bulk of his fortune came from his holdings of metropolitan land. Indeed, our best evidence yet on this topic is for the Windy City in Homer Hoyt's *One Hundred Years of Real Estate Values in Chicago.*

Conversely, of course, one can lose a fortune speculating in real estate. One successful company will never buy a tract unless they are prepared to develop it at once; they speak scornfully of those who are "land poor." Not every site turns out to be State and Madison in Chicago. A patch of ground in downtown Winnipeg had about the same dollar value in 1882 that it has today, while the dollar value of most commodities has risen seven or eight times. How to go broke.

52 ANECDOTE

A Texan was in Puerto Rico on business. Driving a rented car, air conditioned of course, he crossed the island and was appalled at the tiny farms. When he spotted a *jibaro* in a field near the highway, he stopped, noting that even the vines reaching upward from what he took to be yams were staked individually toward the sun.

Texan: "This truck garden just for your own use, Ah reckon."

Farmer: "No, señor, is a living for my family."

Texan: "Shucks, back home I can drive my car all day without ever leavin' mah own propitty."

Farmer: "Si, señor, I had car like that once. *Adios.*"

ITS RELEVANCE

This story achieves two purposes. It deflates the braggadocio of the Texan. By exhibiting the native shrewdness of the Puerto Rican hick, it counters the slanders both against dark-skinned peoples and against inhabitants of the countryside.

ANECDOTE

Charleston, South Carolina, so residents of the eighteenth century might have told you, is where the Ashley River joins the Cooper to form the Atlantic Ocean.

ITS RELEVANCE

A Carolina planter at that time might also have admitted that the Low Country was "a Heaven in spring, a Hell in summer, and a Hospital in autumn."

A common response was to leave before Hell arrived; Newport, Rhode Island was a favorite summer resort. These planters of South Carolina could afford to take prolonged vacations. First, they did not reside on their plantations anyway; nearly all were merchants and/or lawyers and lived in the metropolis, leaving the supervision of their rice paddies and indigo crops to overseers. The Carolina grandees were certainly the richest men in America on the eve of the War for Independence. One man, Henry Middleton, had an estate of 800 black slaves and 50,000 acres. "The planters," observed a member of that select group in 1750, "are full of money." With wealth comes vanity.

ANECDOTES

American visitor looking at the Parthenon:

"The design's OK, but the maintenance is awful."

Easterner looking at Grand Canyon:

"What a great place to throw your old razor blades."

THEIR RELEVANCE

The latter remark is attributed to the late Ring Lardner. He wrote some great short stories, but his satire here seems a bit off center. Admittedly, there are beer cans along the highways across the land, and Americans go to Athens who never heard of the Acropolis. But the typical tourist from the United States off in Europe probably does not deserve to be called a vulgar pig. He is more likely to be Dodsworth.

ANECDOTE

An enormous American car with Illinois plates drove up to a gas station in Banff, Alberta, in the summer. The province of British Columbia is a half hour's drive farther west. After the tank had been filled, the driver had a question.

Driver: "Is there some place around here where I can change my Canadian money for British pounds? We're going on to British Columbia."

Attendant: "Yessir, but it'll be a little out of your way. You know that highway you just came off of, the Trans-Canada? Get back on that and head east until you come to Ottawa; that's our capital. You can't miss it. I'm sure they can fix you up."

Driver: "Thanks a lot for your help."

ITS RELEVANCE

Driving time from Banff to Ottawa: Allow four days, maybe five. Some Canadians shuttle between two attitudes toward the United States. One moment they are ready to fight against the giant south of the border which is seizing control of their country. "You come up here and take good jobs away from Canadians." When in this temper, they don't talk about Lorne Green or John Kenneth Galbraith or Robert Goulet or Raymond Massey. Their other mood is to chortle at that bumptious fool Uncle Sam.

Still, American ignorance about Canada is startling. Probably not 10 per cent of the readers of this book could locate Calgary to within 500 miles. American ignorance of the United States is also startling. So is Canadian ignorance of Canada. In a sampling of classes at the University of Calgary, fewer than half of the students have seen an ocean. Thus they have never been to Vancouver, 675 miles away.

ANECDOTE

Two residents of Evanston, Illinois, both stock brokers, almost inevitably rode the commuter train together down to the Loop. They were close friends, but much badinage passed between them because Jim was Protestant while Don was Catholic. One morning when they met on the platform Don was clearly troubled.

Don: "Jim, I was awake all night because I know that I've lost my faith."

Jim: "Then you'll be coming over to us?"

Don: "Jim, I said that I lost my faith—not my mind."

ITS RELEVANCE

Religion is the pole star around which ordinary Americans have oriented themselves from 1607 to the present. Any blow to a vital part of their creed can upset their total balance. When the Catholic Church gave up the Latin mass and other traditional elements in its ceremonial, what was the effect on the self-picture of thousands or millions of parishioners?

As one ex-Lutheran commented informally in 1966: "The search for identity these days reminds me of a scavenger hunt."

ANECDOTE

Two young rangers in the National Park Service were about to leave headquarters on their first assignment at a line shack (as a rancher would call it) above the 8,000-foot mark in Yosemite. At the last minute the director called them into his office; he and they knew that they would almost certainly be snowed in for the winter. The director handed them a carefully wrapped parcel.

Director: "Men, before this winter ends, you'll hate each other. You'll turn nasty and vicious, until you snap at each other like mad dogs. You'll both be thinking all the time, 'Why isn't there somebody to talk to besides this dumb clout?' When you can't stand it any longer, open this box. In it you'll find gin and vermouth. As soon as you have made your first martini, some son of a bitch will wander out of the woods to tell you that you didn't do it right."

ITS RELEVANCE

The martini is far and away the favorite American cocktail. But formulae for it vary greatly. Peter J. D. Wiles, English, now professor of Soviet economics at the University of London, always went to the kitchen for the vermouth bottle, brought it to the living room, and diluted his to a ratio of 1 to 1. To a Brit, that is a proper martini. To an American it is bilge.

The ritual of pre-dinner cocktails was memorialized by the late Bernard De Voto in *The Hour* (1951).

ANECDOTE

A Boston dowager was trying to be friendly to an out-of-towner at a luncheon party.

Bostonian: "Where are you from?"

Visitor: "Idaho."

Bostonian: "These differences in pronunciation are funny. Here we call it 'Ohio'."

ITS RELEVANCE

A variant has the last word as 'Iowa.'

Geographical ignorance has not disappeared, and it is not limited to Bostonians. Around 1963 many students at Brandeis University thought that the United States ended at the Hudson River. Some acknowledged that it began again at Daly City, California as you approach San Francisco. Certainly they knew more about the layout of Tel Aviv or Florence than of Kansas City or even Jackson, Wyoming.

Differences in pronunciation are indeed funny, however. When I was a boy, I thought there were two distinct states: 'Arkansas' as it was spelled, and 'Arkansaw' as I had always heard it pronounced. To natives of West Virginia, the Kanawha River is the 'Kanoy.' The Crowninshield family of colonial Massachusetts was called 'Grounsell.'

The elderly Mr. Forbes had become quite a trial to his kin-folk in Boston. The old man had taken to hanging out on the steps of the Statehouse, in the shadow of the golden cod, and berating members of the General Court for all sorts of alleged crimes. At last the ruling generation in the family determined that their erring relative needed psychiatric help. They engaged a therapist, warning him that the delinquent would blow a gasket if he learned that he was a mental patient. It was decided that the psychiatrist would pretend to be a scholar engaged in writing a history of the Commonwealth, and that in that connection he was eager to get the reminiscences of an eminent citizen whose personal experiences stretched back to the times of Nathaniel P. Banks and the Civil War.

Old Man: "Well, doctor, what do you want to know?"

Psychiatrist: "Why don't you just start with your earliest memories and tell me whatever comes to mind."

Old Man: "In the beginning I created the Heavens and the Earth."

ITS RELEVANCE

Other tales in these pages reflect that strong sense of kin-ship felt by the old families of Boston. Within that small network of interrelated names, none is more revered than Forbes—not Lowell or Saltonstall or Boylston or Eliot or Cabot or Minot or Lawrence. However peculiar the behavior of a Forbes, no relative would take action that might humiliate him publicly.

The wellspring of this forbearance is, of course, an egocentricity and arrogance. It can be amusing.

60 **ANECDOTE**

A Boston matron drove all the way to the Pacific with her husband. When they got back home, she was asked what route they had taken.

"By way of Dedham."

ITS RELEVANCE

Depending on the exact points you measure from, Dedham is about fifteen miles from Beacon Hill. Between Dedham and the San Francisco Bay, everything wearied this lady. She saw nothing, heard nothing, learned nothing.

Boston has boasted that it is the Hub City—the central sun around which the universe turns. A wonderful spoof is a map of the United States that shows Boston as occupying about two thirds of the geographical area. Texas barely exists.

A Boston spinster, age sixty-nine, lived with her mother, age ninety-one, on Beacon Hill up behind the Statehouse. They lived genteely but penuriously from a small trust fund that had been left to the mother by her great-grand uncle. Most of their hours were spent sitting veiled behind their shabby genteel to watch the flow of traffic, both motor and pedestrian.

Mother: "I can't bear to see these strangers around all the time."

Spinster: "But mother, many of them are tourists, and they spend a great deal of money in the shops about. Mr. Wharton at the bank was telling me just the other day that they are really very important to the economy of Beacon Hill."

Mother: "Can't they just send the money?"

ITS RELEVANCE

Jokes about Boston are more likely to be in-group jokes than those about, say, Texas. They are spawned by Bostonians laughing at the foibles of other Bostonians (or even at their own class in Boston).

Boston in 1974 still has its established aristocrats—families that reach back for two centuries or more—more than any other city in the United States. It seems to contain the last survivors of an ancient occupation: the private trustee; that is, men who as individuals manage trust funds for widows, spinsters, and orphans. But, as the following pages will illustrate, heirs with little capital are likely to find themselves in straitened circumstances.

62   **ANECDOTE**

Since Boston does have an (almost incestuous) community of Brahmins, members of this privileged group are tolerated in their eccentricities. An annual event at Harvard is the dinner to receive new members of the faculty and their wives. At one such occasion a veteran wife turned to the feminine newcomer seated beside her.

Veteran: "Well, Mrs. Johnson, how do you like it here?"

Newcomer: "Oh, fine, just fine. But some things do seem a little bit strange."

Veteran: "Strange? How's that?"

Newcomer: "Well—take that elderly gentleman sitting down the table with his umbrella opened over his head."

Veteran: "Oh, that's not strange. That's just Mr. Shattuck."

ITS RELEVANCE

Under the terms of its original charter dated 1636, Harvard College is legally owned by seven men, including the president and treasurer, who form a self-co-opting body. When a member retires or dies, the survivors choose his successor. The Shattucks, like the Lamonts, have long had their traditional family seat in the Corporation. Twenty years ago one member, Lemuel Shattuck, could be seen walking around the campus in summer wearing a Panama hat. The straw had torn, so he had mended it with Scotch tape.

Mr. Shattuck was a private trustee. Some ten years after the mended straw hat, Mr. Shattuck approached senility. But no respectable Bostonian would say so publicly. By law, no assets could be bought or sold for any estate that he held in trust without his signature—which he could not give. So the prestigious Boston law firm of Ropes, Gray used much of the time of a junior partner to make appearances in court to ask for permission to waive Mr. Shattuck's signature.

ANECDOTE

One summer evening Mr. Lowell had to work late at his office, and he did not feel like taking the next commuter train from Boston to Manchester where his family was vacationing. He would have dinner at his club and stay at the family's flat on Beacon Hill.

After dinner, as he was strolling across the Common, he was accosted by a woman. Embarrassed, he hastily brushed past her. A few paces later he turned to look back. She turned at the same moment, and a gaslight illuminated her face. Horrors, it was Miss Cabot.

He: "Abigail, whatever has brought you to this?"

She: "Uncle Jeremiah, it was either this or dip into capital."

ITS RELEVANCE

For centuries Bostonians have wallowed in trust funds, insurance policies, and government bonds. No sin was worse than squandering your estate, not even converting to socialism or prostitution.

A lady from Boston went to San Francisco to visit her dear friend from Wellesley College days. The two had not met since the Californian removed to the West Coast twenty years earlier. So the first day, the two ladies went out to lunch at one of the city's finest restaurants to have a celebration. The hostess ordered crabmeat salad.

Bostonian: "Aren't you afraid to eat shellfish so far from the ocean?"

ITS RELEVANCE

From the foundation of New England, its foremost men— and many of its anonymous men—had been intensely involved with alien places. But its women were homebound. A Boston dowager regarded it as a daring undertaking when she ventured outwards as far as the South Shore (Plymouth perhaps or Cape Cod) or the North Shore (Essex County, especially Cape Ann). When a woman left Massachusetts, she left for good, usually with husband or family.

But not always. The Dolly Copp Campground in the White Mountains of New Hampshire is named for a farm woman of those parts. To commemorate her silver wedding anniversary, she invited in her children and grandchildren plus a fair sprinkling of other relatives. By 4 in the morning she was up baking mincemeat pies and fixing Indian pudding. While everybody else was swilling up the succulent noontime dinner, she went upstairs, packed her valise, and jammed her hat down on her head. Returning to the dining room, she announced:

"Twenty-five years is long enough to be married to any man. I'm leaving."

She went to Ohio, remarried, and had a few more children.

65 ANECDOTE
Bostonian: "Travel? Why should I? I live here."

ITS RELEVANCE
Q.E.D.

A man stood on Boston Common trying to cross Beacon Street to get to the Statehouse of Massachusetts. Whenever he poked a foot into the gutter, a speeding car almost amputated it. At last he saw a pedestrian on the other side of the street.

Frustrated stranger: "How'd you get over there?"
Bostonian: "Born over here."

ITS RELEVANCE

Americans will argue forever about which region has the worst drivers. A quip tells us: "Driving a car is the other thing that no American male can admit he does badly."

I heard one nearly tragic story from a great student of American history, Ray Allen Billington, about another, Merle Curti. Curti, doing research at the Henry E. Huntington Library, was invited to the University of California at Los Angeles to a social occasion. He does not drive at all, and Mrs. Curti is frightened of driving on freeways. But the only mode of going from San Marino to Westwood is by thruway; there are no routes that use only city streets. The distance is a mere twenty miles, but Mrs. Curti was not positive which exit ramp to take. She stopped at the entrance to the cloverleaf to ponder the situation, and before she knew it three cars had hit hers. Nobody was seriously hurt.

On dozens of highways, cars drive sixty miles per hour with clearance of thirty feet fore and aft with two feet on each side. The phrase "traffic hazard" is far too mild.

ANECDOTE

Little Amy Hallowell, aged 9, was invited to spend a weekend with her rather distant relations the Lowells at their country home outside Boston. Her pleasure at the sojourn was rather confounded when on her first morning there she was asked to say grace at breakfast. Tongue-tied among comparative strangers, but sensing that she must perform, she resorted to the Lord's Prayer:

Our Father, who art in Heaven,

Hallowed be Thy name.

When she returned home, her parents of course asked what she had done. She told of her confusion at breakfast and how she had solved it, concluding: "I told them of course that at home we say

"Hallowell be Thy name."

ITS RELEVANCE

This yarn was told to me by the late David M. Potter, quite possibly the most intelligent man writing about American history in recent times. I have often been attracted to the notion that no listener could fully savor a regional joke unless he has been steeped in the folkways of the region. But Potter chuckled delightedly as he drawled out this one, yet he had never spent much time around Boston: born and reared in Georgia, he had taught at Yale (New Haven emphatically is not Boston) and in California.

Boston is one of the few localities in the United States to have this sort of family pride and self-involvement, outside of the South. Where it exists, it deeply alters the tone of civic affairs. As an insolent wag put it:

Drink up a toast to Boston

The home of the bean and the cod,

Where the Lowells speak only to Cabots,

And the Cabots speak only to God.

ANECDOTE

A lifelong resident of Portland, Maine died at the age of eighty-three. When his estate was probated, it was learned that he had become a millionaire. The local comment was

"Must have had a powerful savin' woman."

ITS RELEVANCE

With the possible exception of the swamp at Jamestown, Virginia, New England may be the worst possible spot in North America for immigrants from Europe to found settlements. But they did. Two hundred years after the first colonies were formed, the common saying was that New England had only two crops it could export: rocks and ice. This indictment is somewhat exaggerated. It always had codfish for shipment, especially to the Catholic countries of the Mediterranean. It produced timbers, naval stores, and finished ships for sale in England. Another export was "chemicals," which on close examination turn out to be potash and pearl ash for use in making candles or soap. The stumps in a wooded region were certainly pesty, but they could be turned into a commodity.

When all that has been said, it remains true that Maine did not boast of many millionaires. It is likewise true that of the trinity of virtues celebrated by the myth of the self-made man in America—industriousness, sobriety, and saving—the one most honored in New England was thrift.

A historian native to Georgia published a study entitled *An Impartial History of the Civil War. From A Southern Point of View.*

In 1900 Barrett Wendell, a professor of English at Harvard University, brought forth *A Literary History of America.* Fred Lewis Pattee commented later that it should have been called *An Intellectual History of Harvard College* (with glimpses at the inferior provinces).

THEIR RELEVANCE

Even as an intellectual history of Harvard, Wendell's book was pathetically defective. But the smugness that he embodied has never died. One of his successors at Harvard, the late Perry Miller, collected in 1954 a volume labelled *American Thought: Civil War to World War I.* Of thirteen authors represented, all except Thorstein Veblen were identified with the Boston or New York City metropolitan areas; half with Harvard. When I tackled a rather analogous task in 1961, seven of the twelve essays were written by men west of the Hudson River. To a certain coterie on the Atlantic littoral, concentrated around the Ivy League campuses, no significant thinking occurs in the hinterlands.

Alger Hiss, a second-level New Dealer, was convicted in 1950 of perjury for denying that he had ever been a Communist agent. He was a summertime resident of Thetford, Vermont. Soon after his conviction, another transient, an ardent Republican, went into Thetford Center to get a haircut.

Visitor in chair: "Well, what do you think of your Alger now?" Barber is thoughtful, while he goes snip, snip, snip. At last:

"Always behaved himself around here."

ITS RELEVANCE

This one came from Edward C. Kirkland, past president of the Economic History Association, at a meeting of the Association at Bryn Mawr College in 1953. Kirkland is both a superb raconteur and a summer resident of Thetford.

We should all be appalled at how many crimes are committed in some other county, in the presence of few witnesses— or none. Hiss's conviction was one of the chief episodes in the concerted effort, dating roughly from 1947 to 1960 (it was *not* the McCarthy era) to tarnish anybody who thought that the social ethics of 1750 could stand improvement.

The significance of the yarn of course is that the Vermont barber had the common sense to adhere to the ancient Scottish verdict: "Not proven."

ANECDOTE

During World War II, a dowager living in a Houston suburb made it a practice to invite a few servicemen on every holiday to have dinner at her home. With this mission of mercy in mind, she telephoned Camp Wallace which put her in touch with the duty officer. She explained the invitation, and got a delighted acceptance. Almost as an afterthought, she said: "Since it is Christmas, please don't send any Jews." "Oh, no, m'am, I'll be sure."

Promptly at 1 p.m. on Christmas, the lady's doorbell rang, and a maid answered it. Three black soldiers were standing self-consciously on the porch. Sensing trouble, the maid went for her mistress. She came, and reeled.

"There must be some mistake."

"M'am, I don't hardly think so. Captain Ginsburg don't make any mistakes."

ITS RELEVANCE

Even while supposedly (and in fact) fighting to destroy the genocidal government of Nazi Germany, the armed forces of the United States continued in countless units to practice blatant racial and religious bigotry. It was not erased by President Truman's over-advertised Executive Proclamation that "ended" racial discrimination in 1948. Twenty-five years later, Negroes in the navy were rebelling by the dozens against bias by their officers, notably on the aircraft carrier *Constellation* stationed at San Diego. Public opinion in the United States had moved to the point that they were not executed for mutiny.

"If it moves, salute it.
"If it don't move, pick it up.
"If you can't lift it, paint it."

ITS RELEVANCE

Feigned humor from World War II is likely to be jejune ribaldry if not outright vulgarity. But the American armed forces did produce several outstanding pieces of wit and folk-sayings.

The above formula for survival seems to have originated with black "service battalions" (call them conscript-labor units) that built bridges, constructed air strips, and so on. Besides this one, Negroes thought up other notable jokes. Here is a jest from the Italian campaign:

A civilian war correspondent was conducting interviews with the residents of Rome to hear their reactions to black American soldiers.

"Oh, they're fine, but those white scum they brought with them are terrible."

This yarn has foundation in fact. A Flying Fortress wing stationed near Oxford, England spent many off-duty hours drinking beer and throwing darts at a nearby tavern. Nightly fracases took place between white fly-boys and black soldiers from a service battalion. The English publican solved the problem by banning all white Americans from his premises.

GRAFFITI AND BUMPER STICKERS

Agamemnon loves Clytemnestra (from a men's room at Brandeis University. Where else?).

Support mental health or I'll kill you.

Jesus Saves
   But Moses invested

Kill Commies
   sponsored by the Campus Crusade for Christ

Spiro Agnew saves Green Stamps ʻ

Mary Poppins is a junkie

Tomorrow has been cancelled for lack of interest

No Easter. They found the body (from a subway stop in Chicago).

THEIR RELEVANCE

Graffiti ("scratchings" from the Italian) doubtless date from the beginnings of written history. But those I remember from my boyhood were nothing more than mindless seven-year-old vulgarities. Since about 1960 a great deal of wit has been expended on these latrine-wall scribbles.

They say quite a bit about the preoccupations of a society. In Puerto Rico I saw a bumper sticker that read

"Cortesia es Contagiosa."

A few days later in Waltham, Massachusetts, the car of one of my neighbors proclaimed

"Protect your right to own and bear arms."

At a protest on the Statehouse lawn in Sacramento against Governor Reagan's proposed increase in student fees, a bumper sticker was held aloft as a poster:

"Support your local police. Bribe a cop today."

Hopefully, nobody ever put that one on his car.

Yea, though I walk through the valley of the shadow of death, I shall fear no evil, because I'm the meanest mother-fucker in the valley.

ITS RELEVANCE

Howard K. Dammond is vice president of Blackside, Inc., a Boston company that makes films and film strips about Negroes in America, their past and present. When I quoted to him this inscription from the men's washroom in a tavern on Woodward near Warren in Detroit, he agreed that it was as obscene and blasphemous as anything he had ever heard. He also agreed that, for its combination of religiosity and antisocial filth, it said volumes about the mood of blacks in Detroit right after the great riots of 1967.

He did suggest, however, that the word "meanest" should be stricken and the word "baddest" written above it.

ANECDOTE

Two young black males in Charleston agreed that they just had to break out of the local cage for a few days. Having saved their money assiduously, they took the bus to the nation's capital and checked into a hotel. After a long ride on a sweltering bus, they wanted a drink in the worst way, but it was Sunday and they had neglected to tuck a bottle into their luggage. They called for a bellhop and asked if he could fix them up. "Sure, no sweat. That'll be $10."

When he returned with the bourbon, they wondered if he could get them a couple of women. "Take half an hour or more. A buck for me now. You can settle up with them." He left on his errand. One stud promptly stripped down to his undershorts and sprawled on the bed holding his drink. His friend remained dressed to answer the door.

Came a discreet rap. When he opened the door, he spun hastily toward the bed.

"Hey, man! These chicks is white."

"Aw brother relax. We just wanna screw 'em, we don't wanna go to school with 'em."

ITS RELEVANCE

When the Supreme Court ruled in a far too verbose judgment that segregation by race in the public schools was a violation of the Constitution and must be (some day) ended, the event inspired several ironic stories. Perhaps none seeks to reverse the past so neatly as the one above.

We all know the traditional refuge of racists: "You wouldn't want your daughter to marry one, would you?" Within months after the decision in *Brown* v. *Board of Education of Topeka* (1954) the conventional preoccupation with sexual relations had been overshadowed by agitation about whether a black guy and a white guy, both age 9, should sit in the same classroom.

Class-
Conscious
Jokes

A runaway slave was captured by a Federal marshal in Pennsylvania. He did not deny that he was the fugitive in question; nonetheless he had to be taken before a court for a ruling on whether he should be extradited back to Virginia.

Judge: "Are you the slave Willie from Virginia?"

Fugitive: "I's the ex-slave Willie from Virginia."

Judge: "Why did you run away, Willie? Did your owner beat you?"

Fugitive: "Aw, naw, Judge, massuh nevuh do a thing like that."

Judge: "Didn't you get enough to eat?"

Fugitive: "Shoah, allus git plinty to eat."

Judge, having more than a little knowledge of how the economics of the situation were prompting a steady export of slaves from Virginia and other border states to the Gulf states: "Were you afraid that your owner would sell you away from your wife and children?"

Fugitive: "Din't have no wife er childurn."

Judge: "Willie, I'm puzzled. Why did you run away?"

Fugitive: "Jedge, thet job still theah ef'n yuh wanna go esk for it."

ITS RELEVANCE

Voluminous disputes have raged for decades about the conditions of life of the slaves. Certainly it is good to learn whatever we can about their food, their lodging, their pace of work, the care for their health. But when we ask about the degree of "slave breeding" or the relative proportions of kindly and brutal masters, we inquire where we will not find answers. Similarly when we ask about the effects of slavery on the psychology of the blacks, we bark up the wrong tree, at least if we use the techniques employed by Stanley Elkins in *Slavery* (1959).

This anecdote sweeps away much of this dross. No matter how decent the intentions of the master, slavery was brutalizing for him and even more so for his slaves.

ANECDOTE

A common laborer on a construction site made a practice
of walking with his wheelbarrow upside down. This peculiarity
earned him the name of Dumbbell Willie. One day he became
so exasperated that he lost his self-control and explained:
"Whenever I turn it right side up, some boss puts something
heavy in it."

ITS RELEVANCE

Such eulogies to folk wisdom should be seen as the con-
verse of the countless yarns that deride formal education. In
the lexicon of university students in the mid-twentieth century:

B.S.   equals   Bull Shit

M.S.   equals   More Shit

Ph.D.   equals   Piled higher and Deeper

Broadly speaking, the slander is valid.

Construction sites give rise to many memorable anecdotes
that are not jokes. A reporter went around about 1940 to interview workers who were building the Cathedral of St. John the
Divine in Manhattan. He talked to three bricklayers, to ask
them what they were doing. One said that he was working to
support his family. The second replied as if he thought the
question was stupid beyond belief: He was laying bricks. The
third was building a monument to the immortality of Christ
our Savior.

Rockefeller Center in Manhattan was built prior to World War II, before earth-moving equipment and fork lifts and mammoth cranes had become commonplace. A guard who worked the swing shift (4 p.m. to midnight) became increasingly suspicious of a laborer who was always leaving just as the guard came on duty. Every afternoon the man would leave pushing his wheelbarrow filled with straw. The guard daily would scratch through the straw, finding nothing. He turned the wheelbarrow upside down. Nothing. But he could not forget the laborer's shifty eyes or his furtive manner. Before the skyscrapers were finished, the laborer retired to live on his Old Age Benefits. On the last day when he was leaving the site with his personal effects

Guard: "Look, I know you been stealing. I ain't never been able to catch you at it. Now you're all through, and nobody can do a thing to yuh. But I'm still curious. Why don't you tell me what you been stealing."

Laborer: "Wheelbarrows."

ITS RELEVANCE

Historians have made a great to-do about strikes, about trade unions, about the confrontations on the bricks. Violence bemuses them. From the Luddites to the Industrial Workers of the World, they love to write about industrial sabotage. But probably the most common technique that individual employees have used to even the score against their bosses has been theft. They might "dog it" or "goldbrick," withholding labor for which they will be paid. Or they might simply develop sticky fingers. Stealing wheelbarrows is not likely to build an estate worth more than a pittance. But if you can tuck under your belt a tiny electronics part worth several hundred dollars, you can amass a tiny fortune.

ANECDOTE

Two maggots, brothers, chanced to be lodged in the same lump of clay that clung to a ditchdigger's spade as he trudged homeward one afternoon. As the clay dried, the clump fell off. One maggot tumbled through a crack in the pavement onto a parched piece of earth. The other fell into a fertile patch of horse manure. As the days went by, one brother prospered. The other could not find anything to eat, until he at last was dying. As he lay gasping with agony, he looked up through the crack in the pavement just as his thriving brother was oozing across it.

Dying maggot: "Brother, how can this be? You up there, so fat that you've got parasites growing in the creases on your belly. Me down here, dying of hunger and thirst."

Opulent brother: "Brains, hard work, and personality."
He leered downward as he spoke the words.

ITS RELEVANCE

This one came from the late Carl Sandburg in a steakhouse in Chicago early in 1942. He then played and sang "Sam Hill."

The restaurant, a favorite of newspapermen, was around the corner from the Tribune Tower. Tiny, it had two items on the menu, broiled steak or broiled chicken, with baked potato and salad. Period. Everything guaranteed superb. Not a bad idea.

ANECDOTE

In 1940 Joe Louis, Negro and heavyweight champion of the world, was to fight Billy Conn, white and outweighed by about forty pounds. Conn was noted for a technique that had first been made famous by Gene Tunney twenty years earlier when he was training for his bout against Jack Dempsey; he practiced running backwards. (Even in wars, this is sometimes a sound strategy: the Russians used it against Napoleon and Hitler; Washington against the English.) Reporters asked Louis how he planned to cope with this diversionary device.

"He can run, but he can't hide."

ITS RELEVANCE

In spite of overwhelming evidence to the contrary, the stereotypes persist about "another dumb jock." Joe Louis was not an especially articulate man, but what of the great center who played basketball for more than a decade for the Boston Celtics, Bill Russell, another black man? At last he became the team's coach. Under a white coach, they had been perennial champions of the world. The first year under Russell, they were not, and word spread in Beantown: These jigaboos can run and jump and shoot, but they can't think. The next year the Celtics were back on top. A reporter went to interview the coach.

Newsman: "You proved long ago that you were the greatest center in basketball, and now it seems you're the best coach. What's your next goal?"

Russell: "Man, I never think about it. I *know* who I am."
Russell also spelled out how white coaches used black players: "When you're at home, start two. On the road, start three. If you're behind, play five."

ANECDOTE

One September two tailors met on the sidewalk on Thirty-third Street in Manhattan's garment district. They paused to exchange hellos and to gossip.

"What's happened to Abe? Haven't seen him for ages."

"Abe? He was in the hospital for a long time, and last week he died."

"Died? Abe died? What a shame, and him so young. And in the middle of the season!"

ITS RELEVANCE

Many urban middle-class Americans think about seasonality of employment only in terms of Back-to-School Specials or "the Christmas rush" or Mother's Day. But for blue-collar workers in many industries it is one of the harshest of all realities.

For decades the auto plants in Detroit simply shut down for months in the summer and autumn because the companies were introducing their new models in the spring. This practice made no sense, since the normal peak market for cars is in the spring anyway, new models or not. One of the few good things to be said for the National Recovery Administration (1933–35) is that it forced General Motors and Ford to bring out their novel delights in the fall of each year. So much for the wisdom of business bureaucrats; authority must make them do what is in their best interest.

Probably bureaucrats in government are no more intelligent than those in corporations. Senator Huey Long said that NRA really stood for Nuts Running America. He was right.

ANECDOTE

A specific waiter in Cleveland made it a practice never to give a customer what he had requested. Not once in thirty years did he get an order straight. Since his establishment was one of the few decent places to eat in all of downtown, he continued to have patrons, but they were sure he was both deaf and stupid. At last he died. One jester remarked:

"At least God could get His message through loud and clear."

ITS RELEVANCE

In the United States, personal service has generally been regarded as demeaning. It is so regarded also in Puerto Rico. Waiters strike back with one of the few weapons they have, even if it means foregoing a tip.

This valuation is far from universal. La Côte d'Azur in Vancouver is staffed by men from France or Switzerland. They never ask whether the food is satisfactory; they know it is superb. They do not hover over you. But a guest finds it impossible to light his own cigarette, and the water glass is never empty, nor is the butter dish.

Mrs. Ginger had a great uncle Zio (Italian for uncle) who immigrated to New York City around the turn of the century when he was seventeen years old. He worked there in fine restaurants for fifty years until he retired. His career as a waiter did not seem to him degrading in any way. He had pride and he had dignity.

A Detroit businessman had been buying new Fords every couple of years from the same dealer. Then his income rose to the point where he could afford a Cadillac, so he thought: Why not? He bought the car. When he had driven only a few blocks from the agency he heard a rattle. He went back and explained the problem. The sales manager announced in a haughty voice: "Cadillacs do not rattle."

Furious, the man drove his Cadillac to the Ford agency where they knew him. They scoffed at him for deserting them, but agreed to check out the problem. Having test driven the car, and rocked it back and forth by hand for a minute, and squirted around with an oil can, they concluded that the noise was coming from within a door.

Service manager: "We'll have to open up the upholstery."
Owner of car: "If you must, you must."
They did. There inside the door was a half pint milk bottle of the type sold by caterers' carts inside factories. The bottle held a coiled note. They fished out the note and opened it. It read:

"Here is that rattle, you filthy rich bastard."

ITS RELEVANCE

This yarn is a direct rebuff to the analysts who deny the presence of class conflict in America. Equally important, it points to the horrible monotony of the assembly line (set down in print by Harvey Swados in his *Man on the Line*). The trim shop at Dodge held two parallel lines. Along them worked 3,500 men. A day held two types of excitement. Each of the massive supporting columns for the roof was plastered every morning with the crossword puzzle from the *Free Press,* and I was pestered all day for answers to silly questions about which I had not the slightest idea. The real quivers, however, were set off by the appearance of a female friend of mine. She was chief steward in the wire room, which gave her some freedom of movement. As she came through the door, every wrench in that mausoleum would start to whomp on a car body. Now you know where some of those dents on your car came from. At least on a 1948 Dodge.

The Air Force, gung ho to smash the sound barrier, had·
used a large and prestigious team to design a new fighter
plane. Day came for the test flight, before a grandstand
loaded with dignitaries. The plane came booming down, the
wings ripped off, it crashed.

One ranking executive, as he was gloomily leaving the
bleachers, overheard a little man in grimy coveralls muttering:

"Perforations. Use perforations."

A new team of specialists was assembled to work out a new
design. Again: the same scene. Again, the same result: the
wings ripped off. Again, the same little man in grimy clothes
(the same coveralls?) muttering:

"Perforations. Try perforations."

The general hurried to catch the little man. At his suggestion,
on the third model they put perforations where the wings
joined the fusilage. Needless to say, the location and dimen-
sions of these holes were worked out to tolerances that might
as well have been an angstrom. Came the test flight, the plane
zoomed down, it pulled out of the dive, the wings held. As the
pilot was landing the exuberant general seized the little man
and shook him with delight, shouting:

"How did you do it? How did you solve a problem that our
finest physicists and mathematicians and aeronautical engineers couldn't solve?

Little man: "It was easy. I get awful dirty at work, so at quit-
ting time I go wash up. Then I pull out a paper towel to dry off.
It never rips where there are perforations."

ITS RELEVANCE

Never listen to experts. Trust in the common man.

An American car manufacturer was eager to expand its exports to Mexico. It needed crucial revisions in its import license. After its agent in Mexico City had made the needed appointments, a vice president flew down from Detroit. He was ushered in to see the Minister of Trade. They chatted amiably for a while, then the vice president made his petition clear.

Minister: "I will certainly look into it. We'll see what can be done. Now you must excuse me or I'll be late for a meeting."

Executive: "By the way, through a friend of mine, I can get fine bargains on new Cadillacs."

Minister: "What would a bargain cost?"

Executive: "Fifty dollars."

The Minister of Trade drew a wallet from his breast pocket and passed over $100.

Executive: "I'll give you your change right now."

Minister: "I'll take two."

ITS RELEVANCE

This one should have been recorded by Mark Twain and entitled *Innocents Abroad.* I have long contended that payoffs are inevitable in every government. The United States differs from most countries in a vital respect: whereas in Argentina or Vietnam the tribute is levied by politicians but it leads to no social benefits, in the United States the Massachusetts Turnpike gets built. Somebody should write a dissertation entitled *The Economic Uses of Political Corruption.*

The above illustration came from an executive in the International Bank for Reconstruction & Development (the World Bank).

A group of passengers boarded a Boeing 707 airliner at Dulles Airport outside Washington. Many of them had ridden commuter trains that did not carry locomotive engineers because they were controlled from a central and stationary set of switches. A couple even had toy airplanes whose flight could be controlled from the ground.

After the loading gate had been rolled away and the door to the plane closed, a voice spoke to them through an electronic amplifier:

"Ladies and gentlemen, today you will make history. In the long and gallant history of commercial aviation in America, no plane has ever taken off without a flight crew. But, as the absence of stewardesses may have suggested to some of you, this is an unmanned aircraft. This amazing example of the progressive mentality of Zilch Airlines was suggested to us by the success of earth-controlled capsules in our nation's incredible conquest of outer space, and our program was undertaken entirely in the interests of your safety.

"Ladies and gentlemen, thank you for flying with Zilch Airlines. This has been a recorded announcement. And now, as your plane approaches the runway for takeoff, we wish to assure you that nothing can go wrong . . . go wrong . . . go wrong . . . go wrong . . ."

ITS RELEVANCE

To any thinking person, the assertion that "we have eliminated the human factor and turned events over to computers and other electronic controls . . ."—well, that claim lost all credibility when three astronauts at Cape Kennedy, Florida were cremated in their space ship.

A stationary engineer was called in by a hospital because one of its boilers had ceased to function. When he arrived, the medical director of the institution went to the basement with him. The engineer leaned into the boiler, made one tap with his hammer, pulled his head out, and said: "She should work now." She did. At the end of the month the hospital received a bill for $260.50. The medical director, furious, called in the engineer to protest.

M.D.: "How can you submit such a ridiculous bill?"

Mechanic: "Well, the ten dollars is my regular service fee; that's for making the call. Fifty cents is for that one tap with my hammer. Two hundred fifty dollars is for knowing where to tap."

ITS RELEVANCE

Physicians can get indignant at the notion that a plumber charges $8 an hour. But a brain surgeon thinks nothing of charging $5,000 for an operation. He gets paid for knowing where to cut.

Occupational Jokes

ANECDOTE

Two anthropologists were on a field trip in darkest Africa when they were captured by cannibals. Terrified, they were herded into a compound with the other fresh meat. They still could not escape the professional habits of their adult lives, so they were entranced by a sign that posted current prices:

Professors	$5
Associate professors	$3
Assistant professors	$2
Instructors	$1
Deans	25¢

In their bemusement they summoned a guard to ask why deans were so cheap.

"Is the meat so much tougher than other academics?"

"No, about the same. But have you ever tried to clean one?"

ITS RELEVANCE

The late Carl F. Wittke, dean of the graduate school at Western Reserve during the final many years of his career, was one of the few distinguished academic administrators that I have known. Any graduate student could see him on a whim—between 9 a.m. and noon. In the afternoon Wittke was home writing, as a dozen or so books will testify. He also persisted in teaching every year his course on immigration into the United States. He was not lazy, nor was he care-less, in its pure meaning. When I was a young (badly underpaid) instructor, he looked at me across his desk and said: "You know, Ray, the chief part of my duty is to get you the tools that you need to do your job well." He meant it, and lived by it.

If more deans could grope their ways to a similar attitude, the flock would not have such a bad name.

93   **ANECDOTE**

A Yale man was standing at a urinal when a University of Chicago graduate sauntered in and took the adjacent stall. The Chicago alumnus finished first and headed for the vestibule. The Yale man called contemptuously:

"In the Ivy League they taught us to wash our hands after going to the bathroom."

"That so? Around here we learn not to piss on our hands."

ITS RELEVANCE

Antagonisms between the Big Ten and the Ivy League are notorious. Academically, perhaps the average in the East might run a bit higher, but not so much higher that the law schools at Harvard and Yale and Columbia should oligopolize the clerkships to the Supreme Court of the United States. The "gentleman's C" is after all a recognized phenomenon in Cambridge, Massachusetts. In the Midwest the products of the most famous Eastern men's schools are likely to be regarded as not only snobbish but also effeminate. The next page offers an illustration.

A Yale graduate and a Chicago man went to lunch together several times a week in New York. Both young, they were both customers' men in a stock brokerage firm in Manhattan. They were similar but not identical, as the Easterner became increasingly aware.

Finally one day he blurted out: "I never seem to get anywhere with a woman, while you keep scoring right and left. What's your secret?"

"Nothing much to it. When you meet a woman you find attractive, you ask her to have dinner with you and go to the theater. Then you take her back to your apartment for an after-the-theater supper. I usually serve chicken-in-aspic, but it could be almost anything good. Oh, a fine wine of course. Next you turn on the music. I've got a special switch for the hi-fi under the dining room table, but that's just a gimmick; you don't need it. You ask her to dance. As you're waltzing around, you steer her into the bedroom. Then things either happen, or they don't. If they don't, you look for another chick."

When they next went to lunch, the Chicago man asked:

"How did it go?"

Yaley (sour): "Fine, up to a point."

Chicago: "Hunh?"

Yale: "Well, I danced her into the bedroom, just like you said. Then I was bent over to put my shoetrees into my shoes, and I looked up, and she was gone."

ITS RELEVANCE
Enough said.

ANECDOTE

A professor of English at the University of Chicago was going to Baltimore to do some research. He was a Midwesterner who had acquired a passion for seafood. A gourmet, he had never been to Maryland, so he sought around until he found a native of that state. His colleague told him: "The shellfish is all fine, maybe the crabmeat especially, but what really brings a gleam to the eyes of a Baltimorean is scrod."

The visitor reached his hotel in Baltimore, showered and changed quickly. Dashing out the front door of the building, he flagged down a taxi. "Now I want you to take me some place where I can get scrod."

The cabbie slammed on his brakes and pulled to the curb, where he turned to look at his passenger. "Mister, 19 years I drive a hack in this town, and you're the first guy who ever used the pluperfect subjunctive."

ITS RELEVANCE

This one was told at an annual convention of the Modern Language Association. It is hard to imagine another ambience in which one might hear this particular form of argot.

The story also underscores the frequency with which highly educated people have been forced to accept for sustained periods a job that seems below their capacity. When we made a visit to Boston in the spring of 1970 during a severe cutback in defense expenditures, a local friend explained: "If you hail a cab around here now, the driver probably has a Ph.D. in physics."

ANECDOTE

A copy editor in the office of a book publishing firm on Madison Avenue was trying to explain to an author that his manuscript violated several canons of good grammar. Her patience began to tire as she pointed to split infinitives, prepositions that ended sentences, and so on. At last he grew irritated: "For God's sake, woman, your bloody rules would castrate Shakespeare. Here, I'll give you one that I memorized from a gravestone in Dorset. It breaks a lot of rules, but nobody doubts what it means:

'Us can go to stay with she
'But her can't come to visit we.'"

ITS RELEVANCE

Copy editors tend to resemble those junior high school teachers who make you stand at the blackboard parsing sentences, and who approach poetry by stressing the difference between dactyls and spondees. All such attempts to rigidify and simplify the American language are so many bloodlettings that drain the juices from a flexible and living organism.

Language must change because life changes. A Puritan used the word "invent" where we now say "discover"; "invention" in our sense would have seemed to him the grossest blasphemy because he knew that man could not create anything. That was God's province.

"The free-silver movement," said Henry Demarest Lloyd in 1896, "is the cowbird of reform." Any farm boy then knew that the cowbird took over nests built by other species and threw out their eggs to make way for its own. For ill-repute, the cowbird ranked with the starling. Students of today have never heard of cowbirds and certainly don't know their traits. The metaphor has lost its sting, and this epigram when told in a classroom needs a long-winded explanation that almost kills it.

ANECDOTE

An English teacher was conducting a spell-down. The word was "shift." Teacher says John should spell it aloud, and he does so—properly. But at the blackboard he writes: "Shit." Since the day was Tuesday, the school board psychiatrist was present on his weekly visit, and he promptly went to the teacher of the class to ask if he and John could have a few private minutes in the corridor.

When they returned, the teacher asked John to spell "shift" aloud. He was right. At the blackboard, however, he wrote "S H I T" before he paused to add "E".

Teacher: "See? Before you butted in, he could spell 'shit' correctly."

ITS RELEVANCE
Again, no commentary.

ANECDOTE

In 1943 two millhands from North Carolina were stretched flat on their respective bunks in Camp Stewart. It was lunch break. The site of the installation, some forty miles southwest of Savannah, was as woebegone as any that the army had found—and it had looked hard.

Masters: "Littlefield, what time's it?"

Littlefield: "Twelve fuckin thirty-seven o'clock."

ITS RELEVANCE

The English language might be the most debased coinage in the world. A captain who served in the Philippines in 1945 said that he could top the above anecdote. Having listened to his story, I agreed with him. He was in the rear seat of a jeep, with a driver, on a rainy night. Their engine cut out, and they barely had enough momentum to coast into a military motor pool. Two mechanics came out in slickers and pushed them into a motor bay. One chap went away. The other got a screwdriver and a wrench, lifted the hood, and started tampering. At length he poked his head into the window, saw the officer in the back seat, and announced:

"Fuckin fucker's fucked."

A one-word language, with suffixes. Shakespeare? Milton? Yeats? Forget about them.

ANECDOTE

Two travelers for a college textbook publishing firm (eu-
phemistically called "field editors") were new to the house
when the annual sales meeting came up in September; this
conversation came during coffee break on the first day.

Man #1: "Gee, you must be from the Ivy League."

Man #2: "Dartmouth in fact. How did you know?"

Man#1: "Well, it's your natty clothes, and your talk, and the
way you handle yourself in general."

Man #2: "You're from Utah State."

Man #1: "Gee, howjuh know? Is there something about my
clothes or talk and general air?"

Man #2: "No, I read it off your school ring when you were
picking your nose."

ITS RELEVANCE

This is not the city picking on the country. It is the East
decrying the West. Often with justification. When I was a
Southerner I learned the falsity behind the image of "the hos-
pitable South." Living on the Great Plains, I have come to
believe that they contain the least sociable people in all Creation. On the other hand, the snobbishness of the East is also
a trial and a burden. We are all sinners.

ANECDOTE

An eleven-year-old boy came back from school bearing homework. He was assigned to write a two-page essay about penguins. His mother was out; his father was sweating over his company's budget for the coming year. Boy: "Dad, I need to know something about penguins." Father: "Look in the encyclopedia." Three hours later the boy, looking like he had been caught in a blizzard, staggered downstairs carrying two sheets of paper; he had been snowbound in the famous Eleventh Edition of the *Encyclopaedia Britannica.*

Boy: "Dad."

Impatient Father: "Yes."

Boy: "Dad, that book told me more about penguins than I wanted to know."

ITS RELEVANCE

This yarn pinpoints one of the troublesome problems that confront teachers, writers, and other practitioners in communications. What is the audience like? How much detail do they want? How much detail will they stand for?

This dilemma may be more severe in the United States than in other cultures. Most Americans never think about the query that goes in philosophy under the label: "levels of abstraction." A folk tale among the Blackfoot might tell you in vivid specifics how a wolf appeared; another among the Iroquois will leap to the opposite polarity to describe Manitou, the nebulous Spirit of the Universe. Americans like to dwell in the misty (not very informative) medium: Can sovereignty be divided? Can representation be virtual?

ANECDOTE

A sociologist got a sizable grant in aid of research to study leadership in small groups. Having heard that "real scientists" do pilot projects before spending vast resources, he determined to follow the same course. He caught an ordinary housefly and placed it on his desk under a wire screen with a custom-made door. He cautiously opened the door, grasped one leg of the fly with a pair of tweezers, pulled off the leg, and commanded: "Jump!" When released, the fly jumped. This process continued through four more legs, and each time the command was obeyed. At Stage Six the command failed. Always the scientist, the sociologist wrote in his notebook: "When a fly has lost six legs he becomes deaf."

ITS RELEVANCE

Considering the widespread scorn for sociologists, we may wonder why departments in that field, which have swelled and burgeoned apace, have been such successful imperialists. Certainly the penchant of sociology for meaningless jargon is a loathsome disease of pedantry. But the discipline survives because a smattering of its practitioners have combined solid data with enlightening concepts. Can historians claim more? All academic disciplines are infected by the pompous and the incompetent. Often when they turn against each other it is a case of the pot and kettle calling each other dirty.

Dr. Hugh G. J. Aitken, reared in London and a graduate of St. Andrew's in Scotland, came to the University of Toronto soon after World War II as a graduate student. He was assigned to teach in a survey course on Canadian-American relations. A student came griping about his grade on an examination. Aitken, impeccably reasonable as always, dragged out the paper.

Aitken: "Show me the answer to any one of the four questions, that you think is especially good, and I'll certainly consider raising your grade."

Student (some minutes later): "Here on Question 3, I mention that the filthy Americans burned the capitol at York."

Aitken: "But you don't mention that the British burned Washington."

Student: "Washington? Burned? I thought that he was shot in a theater."

ITS RELEVANCE

Students can make mistakes that, at least to an outsider, seem incredible. Some of them are inadvertent rays of light.

"The American Revolution was spurred by a struggle for elf-government."

The Habsburg dynasty in Austro-Hungary was "the Duel Monarchy."

A fitting conclusion is a typographical mistake that I repeatedly made while teaching myself to be a historian: "the Untied States." When I learned a little about the Civil War, the last one did not make me laugh.

ANECDOTE

A tailor was measuring a prominent movie actress for a fitted custom-made suit in gray flannel. Chalk firmly in hand, he marked her slightly below the top of her breasts.

He: "Here we will put breast pockets."

She: "But I don't want outside pockets."

He (grabbing her bosom in both hands and rubbing vigorously) "All right, no outside pockets."

ITS RELEVANCE

The occupation of tailor has given rise to many jests. A practitioner in Lexington, Kentucky closed a deal with a customer:

"We got just one thing left to settle. Did you all want the inside pocket to be half-pint or pint size?"

ANECDOTE

Two specialists in Near Eastern Studies were standing on Mount Calvary and gazing with rapture at the Cross.

First man: "He was a great teacher."

Second man: "Yeah, but he never published."

ITS RELEVANCE

The punch line has a variant:

Second man: "Yeah, but he never learned how to pull down the big grants."

This variant was most popular among natural scientists during those twenty years after World War II when Federal agencies (Department of Defense, Atomic Energy Commission, NASA, National Institute of Mental Health, and who knows who else) would give a quarter of a million dollars to anybody who could go to the toilet by himself.

This version never made much headway among humble folk in the humanities and social sciences simply because, except for an occasional errant freight, the gravy train did not pass through the piney barrens where they lived.

105 **ANECDOTE**

A certain diamond merchant on West 47th Street phoned the offices of Otis Elevator in New York City. He had a problem; could they please send an engineeer over. They did. After inspecting the situation, the engineer said:

"Not much to it. You want to move your safe to another building up the block, right? Well, the whole thing weighs only a ton and a half, the door amounts to at least two thirds of that, and the elevator will handle 2,500 pounds. So take the door off and you can get it out with no trouble."

That afternoon Otis Elevator got another call from the same diamond merchant, now hysterical. The Otis man hastened back to 47th Street. The merchant had gotten in a crew of workmen, who removed the door of the safe. They put the safe on the elevator, then put the door on top of the safe.

ITS RELEVANCE

This happened in 1957.

ANECDOTE

A motorist got a flat tire. He stopped, removed the lug nuts, and carefully placed the five of them into the hubcap. Unfortunately before he could get the spare tire onto the hub, a strong wind blew the hubcap skittering; four of the lug nuts fell through a grill into a manhole in the highway. Now he really swore a blue streak. A male voice interrupted his profanity. "Hey, mister, here's what you do. Take one lug nut from each of the other wheels and put them on that one. That should at least get you to town where you can buy some more nuts." Straightening up to thank the man for his sound advice, the motorist saw that he was standing behind a sturdy metal fence—bars in fact. About twenty yards down the highway was a gate labeled "Washtenaw County Mental Hospital."

Motorist: "Obviously you have a very quick mind. How did you get in there?"

Inmate: "Aw, buddy, come off it. They put me here because I'm crazy, not because I'm stupid."

ITS RELEVANCE

Driving by the best route from Waltham, Massachusetts to Cambridge, you pass a mental institution that is about the size of a large wheat farm in Montana. It seems to cover half of Middlesex County. By 1960 such establishments were common in every state of the Union.

This joke also highlights the degree to which we permit our language to be bevelled down and eroded away, so that words have lost their cutting edge. We do not distinguish "crazy" from "stupid"—nor either from "ignorant." We cannot tell "earnest" from "serious." Readers are respectfully referred to Mark Twain's "Fenimore Cooper's Literary Offenses."

Two psychiatrists, one elderly, the other youngish, had their respective offices on the same floor in a Medical Arts Building. The younger man grew increasingly envious as he watched his counterpart leave the office day after day at 3 or 4 o'clock with a golf bag on his shoulder. Finally he made bold to ask the older practitioner to join him for a cup of coffee. Accepted.

Young Man: "I realize that you have been in practice a lot longer than I have, but I still don't see how you can afford to quit work so early to go play golf."

Elderly Man: "I did it even when I was younger."

Young Man: "But how do you handle your patients so fast?"

Elderly Man: "How do you handle yours so slow?"

Young Man: "Well, I try to establish some rapport at the start of each session, so that they get started talking, and I listen to what they say, and when they've left I write it out, and then I try to analyze it. Some days I'm here working until midnight."

Elderly Man: "You listen?"

ITS RELEVANCE

In 1947 nobody was anybody until he (or she) had been to a psychoanalyst. Twenty years later, the same function was performed for suburban idlers by the oral surgeons. Once it was fashionable to have your soul scrubbed with harsh soap; then it became the fad to have your gums curettaged.

About 1955 an account executive in an advertising agency on Madison Avenue was being paid $20,000 a year, a handsome salary at that time. It did him little good. He, his wife, and their two children were all undergoing psychoanalysis.

ANECDOTE

Two doctors pass in the corridor of the hospital.
Surgeon: "Good morning."
Psychiatrist (to himself): "Wonder what he meant by that?"

ITS RELEVANCE

The lengths to which psychoanalysts will go—and the depths to which they will sink—were made clear to me on a magical evening in Washington, D.C. in 1950. Present were four M.D.s: two psychiatrists, a pediatrician, and the director of the Public Health Association. One psychiatrist, masculine, got started reading aloud from Eli Wallach's *Hopalong Freud Rides Again*. It was funny enough in itself. But then the qualified members of the gathering began running off to look up pertinent passages in the recent medical journals. If Wallach had possessed these annotations, he might have written an essay even better than the masterpiece that he did produce.

ANECDOTE

A drunk was seen walking around a lamppost, clinging to it in despair. The trauma ended when, after circling the post three or four times, he sagged down onto the curbstone. Propping his face in his hands, he sobbed:

"My God, I'm walled in!"

ITS RELEVANCE

Another instance of free-floating anxieties. People try to endure them—day by day. As Henry David Thoreau remarked: Our brethren live lives of quiet desperation.

A young business consultant in Los Angeles was troubled not only by dreams but also by daytime fantasies. They concerned sexual intercourse with a wide variety of beasts. At length he became so disturbed by his aberrations that he resolved to consult a psychiatrist. He did so.

Psychiatrist: "What exactly are the animals involved?"
Patient: "Often they are sheep."
Psychiatrist: "And—?"
Patient: "A few times a mare or a cow."
Psychiatrist: "And—?"
Patient: "Twice a snake."
Psychiatrist: "Snakes!?"

ITS RELEVANCE

Bestiality, like sodomy and incest, is perhaps more common than the ordinary person can acknowledge. William Bradford left us this record of a 16- or 17-year-old servant in Plymouth, Massachusetts in 1642: "He was this year detected of buggery, and indicted for the same, with a mare, a cow, two goats, five sheep, two calves and a turkey. Horrible it is to mention, but the truth of the history requires it."

A turkey!? The youth and all of the lower animals were executed.

A suburban matron in Shaker Heights, Ohio was so upset by her hallucinations that she went to a psychiatrist. Her problem was that she constantly felt as if insects were tearing at her.

Psychiatrist: "What kind of insects?"

Woman: "Usually spiders, but often bumblebees or yellow jackets, or tiny things that I can't put a name to."

Psychiatrist: "Anything else?"

Woman: "Well, it sounds almost too silly to mention, but also butterflies."

Psychiatrist, slapping frantically at his jacket: "Don't get your butterflies on me."

ITS RELEVANCE

In the years following World War II, the mind doctors were riding a bull market. It was universally believed—except among their patients—that many of them had taken up the occupation because they had severe personal problems of their own. In an exciting metaphor, one woman referred to her former husband, a psychiatrist, as being "emotionally tone-deaf."

ANECDOTE

A Brandeis student went to the Counseling Service at 5:30 one afternoon to complain that he had a screw growing into his navel. Only one psychologist was on duty, and he was going to be late getting home and was supposed to take his wife to a dinner party. He hastily gave advice. "Do you live around here?" "Yes, in Newton." "Do you have a bathtub and a screwdriver?" "Yes."

"Then here's what you do. Go home and fill the bathtub with tepid water, not too hot, not too cold. Put the screwdriver on the floor beside the tub and climb in. Let yourself just hang loose. When you are completely relaxed, pick up the screwdriver and remove the screw. OK?"

The psychologist went home, caught the devil from his wife, and they went to the dinner party. When they arrived there, he was told to phone his answering service. The assistant told him that she had gotten a hysterical call from a young man in Newton. He recognized the name and dialled the number, thinking unprintable thoughts to himself.

"Did you do exactly what I told you to do?"

"Yes, doc, I did, right to the letter. The bath felt great, and I thought everything was going to be fine. But when I took the screw out, my ass fell off."

ITS RELEVANCE

This classic exemplifies what some psychologists call "free-floating anxiety." Some persons need to be worried. If you snatch one worry away from them, they are compelled inwardly to instantly find another. When women were anxious that they might become pregnant, their fears had a relation to reality. But in the modern world, as Franz Kafka so brilliantly illustrated, anxieties may be only fantasies that warp the external world in unpredictable ways.

Sex
Jokes

A young lady showed up in 1925 in a medium-sized town in the Midwest to teach in the high school. She was very attractive, and the bachelors started to scout her out. Their ardor waned when she let it be known that she was also going to teach Sunday School in the First Methodist Church. But one chap who prided himself on being a real stud decided to give it a fling, so he asked her to the movies. She accepted graciously. Going to the picture show they drove past the local tavern. He asked if she wanted a drink since they were going to be early for the movie. Goodness no, she didn't drink. He offered her a cigarette. Goodness no, she didn't smoke. He sat, almost despairing, through the movie. When they were back in the car, the swain determined to gamble hard.

He: "Will you spend the night with me?"

She: "Why, yes, that might be right nice."

The next morning

He: "I can't figure you at all. You won't drink, you don't smoke, but wow, some of the things you dreamed up in the night."

She: "That's what I keep telling my Sunday School classes: You can so have fun without drinking and smoking."

ITS RELEVANCE

This one came to me from Professor Aubrey C. Land of the University of Georgia—a fine spoof on the convolutions and warpings of my parents' morality. Together with ministers' sons, schoolteachers have long been a favorite butt of malicious gibes. My friend Harald Bakken, reared as the son of the superintendent of schools in Aitkin, Minnesota (pop. 2,000), assures me that his status was worse than that of the pastor's boys.

ANECDOTE

A recent bride in 1938 was boasting modestly that she and her husband had bought a spanking new six-room bungalow. What's more, they had furnished the living room entirely by their diligent accumulation of the stamps from bars of soap.

"What about the other five rooms?"

"Oh, that's where we keep the soap."

ITS RELEVANCE

Everybody today is aware of Green Stamps, S & H Stamps, Plaid Stamps, as well as the numerous premiums to be gotten with some cigarette cartons or brands of gasoline. Some do not realize that this is the sort of false economy that can land you in bankruptcy court. The value gained to the consumer in relation to the man-hours used must result in an average wage approximating 7 cents an hour.

I once sublet a beautiful old farmhouse on Cape Cod, Massachusetts. The owner, a Vermonter himself, had learned thrift. In the gigantic pantry he had labelled a drawer with the words: "String too short to use." I made a label for the adjoining drawer on a strip of white adhesive tape: "String too short to save."

At our next meeting, the owner grinned—but he was doubtless bleeding inside.

Learning that a man in the city was about to enjoy his nine-tieth birthday, the *Indianapolis News* about 1940 sent a reporter to interview him. The newsman arrived mid-afternoon to find the old man sitting on his front porch in his rocking chair and smoking a cigar. They chattered for a few minutes.

Reporter: "I see you're smoking a cigar. Do you use many?"

Man: "Don't count. But twelve or so a day I guess."

Reporter: "Do you drink too?"

Man: "Oh, pint or so a day I reckon."

Reporter: "Women?"

Man: "Well, sonny, had me three wives. Fourteen children, twenty-eight grandchildren, reckon by now it's 'bout forty-three great-grandchildren."

Reporter: "Mr. Corey, I am truly surprised. In view of this re-markable record of dissipation, how have you managed to survive for ninety years?"

Man: "Maybe 'cause I never wasted no energy resisting temptation."

ITS RELEVANCE

Nobody will ever know whether this elderly man was so-phisticated enough to understand the implications of his re-marks. But as a spoof of the puritanism that glowered over the nineteenth and twentieth centuries (far different from the seventeenth-century version), this episode seems to me perfect.

Two obvious fairies were walking along Sixth Avenue just above Eighth Street, hand in hand. Immediately ahead of them were a man and his wife, arguing like lunatics. One gay lad said to his friend:

"Do you see, dear? I told you that mixed marriages never work out."

ITS RELEVANCE

Only in limited subcultures was homosexuality a topic for polite conversation until about 1955 or so. A friend of mine in the army in 1944 in Washington, D.C. was a former announcer for one of the national radio networks. When, to amuse himself, he would put on his well-nigh perfect pansy act in a crowded elevator in a downtown office building, his cronies felt sufficiently embarrassed to want to shrink into the floor.

By the time of the Johnson administration, the arrest of a topmost White House aide on charges of homosexuality in the YMCA in Washington did not provoke any notable amount of scandal. It did provoke some jokes.

The President, as part of a much ballyhooed campaign for "economy in government," had made it known that all residents of the Presidential mansion were under strict orders to turn off the lights when they left a room. "Now we know why he *really* wants the lights turned off."

Within two hours after this alleged incident of homosexuality appeared on the front pages of Boston newspapers, I got a long-distance call from a colleague then on leave in Washington. It seems that this slogan had already been invented and put into circulation:

Go either way
with LBJ

ANECDOTE

On another day the same two gay lads were strolling along at the same place on Sixth Avenue. A woman walked past. One man turned to look after her, and he was still motionless, still looking, when she disappeared around the corner into Ninth Street. Turning to his friend, he exclaimed:

"Good Lord, some of them are so beautiful they make me wish I was a Lesbian."

ITS RELEVANCE

Having heard and read about the purported homosexuality of a White House assistant, I remarked:

"You could guess that Lyndon, with his passion for 100 per cent consensus, would go after the homosexual vote as soon as he was told how large it was."

Obviously this comment is far too sweeping. The above story probably goes about as far as "community acceptance" would tolerate in the United States at the present time. And millions would still shriek that community acceptance was far too lenient.

ANECDOTE

A young account executive in a San Francisco advertising agency was much taken by a secretary new to the office. He was a bachelor, but he still had a hang-up. She was a Negro. His upbringing was not blatantly biased, but his parents were moderately prejudiced and he knew it. He could expect some withering remarks if word got out that he had been seen showing a black woman around town.

Still, he cranked up his nerve and asked her to go to dinner with him. "Sure, when do you want to pick me up? I live at 411 O'Farrell." In accord with the arrangements, the young man knocked on the apartment door at the appointed time. His date came to the door wearing sandals, since it was summer, plus a necklace. Nothing more. He gaped.

She (slyly): "You can't go wrong with basic black and pearls."

ITS RELEVANCE

Long ago, in *The Theory of the Leisure Class* (1899), Thorstein Veblen cited instances to show that standards and fashions filter down from those groups that are highest in wealth, income, and prestige. This theory has not been sufficiently tested, but evidence for it seems strong: Dearborn will strive, on a less expensive level, to emulate the rugs and the lamps that are current in Grosse Point Farms.

But the reverse can occur. The heroine of the above story is obviously mocking the clichés that were current around the sororities.

Political
Jokes

Thomas Jefferson was elected President in 1800 by almost the narrowest margin conceivable (1916 and 1960 come to mind). His opponents, who had by now coalesced into the Federalist party, were sure that this Jacobin traitor aimed to revolutionize the country. They also believed that his adherents were a mob of spoilsmen with no intent except to plunder the public treasury. Wrote one New England Federalist to another: "When these gentry find that there are more PIGS than TEATS, what a squealing there will be in the hog pen."

ITS RELEVANCE

Jefferson's election prompted many of the older Federalists to simply withdraw from public life to their country estates. Their younger colleagues might, as David Hackett Fischer shows in his admirable *The Revolution of American Conservatism* (1965), resolve to continue the fray by the new groundrules of a democratizing nation. Some of them, thank goodness, developed a sense of sick humor.

ANECDOTE

In 1850 a phalanx of Southern politicians were orating about secession from the Union. They were undoubtedly serious in considering this course. The crisis resulted in the Compromise of 1850. Although several of its provisions were obnoxious to many Northerners, they were outraged by proposed—more severe—amendments to the Fugitive Slave Act of 1793. Nonetheless, Daniel Webster of Massachusetts gave his famous Seventh of March Speech in support of the proposals.

The reaction of New England's intellectuals was violent. John Greenleaf Whittier tried to be restrained in his poem "Ichabod":

Let not the land once proud of him
  Insult him now,
Nor brand with deeper shame his dim,
  Dishonored brow.

Nothing restrained was apparent in the onslaught by Ralph Waldo Emerson:

"The word 'honor' in the mouth of Mr. Webster is like the word 'love' in the mouth of a whore."

ITS RELEVANCE

Webster, throughout his long career in Congress, can fairly be called shifty and unprincipled. But on this occasion he was right (see next page). He must have known that his commitment would bring curses bouncing off his head in his home state. The episode illustrates the persistent hostility between arm-chair theorizers and men of affairs (prior to about 1830 this hostility was almost unknown; usually the two groups were one). The former can perch on their pedestal of high-minded principle; the latter must clamber down in the mud to cope with daily conflicts. We can be grateful that poets seldom make public policy.

ANECDOTE

John Randolph of Roanoke spoke harshly of a longtime colleague in Congress. Henry Clay, said Randolph, was "like a mackerel in the moonlight; he shines and he stinks."

ITS RELEVANCE

Did Randolph mean that Clay was a pure opportunist? Or rather that Clay was a brilliant orator, a quality in him widely admitted by contemporaries, but that his rhetoric was used for wicked causes? The second choice seems much more likely, since Clay of all the statesmen of his generation held to a fixed set of proposals, so set that they even earned a label of their own. The American System had as its main elements a central bank (the Second Bank of the United States), internal improvements (highways and harbors), and protective tariffs. Each one of these policies was anathema to Randolph, Representative from Virginia almost continuously from 1799 to 1829. In 1826 Clay met Randolph in a duel—fortunately bloodless.

Clay's forthright nationalism, his sense of "saving the Union," prompted him to champion many deals. One was the Compromise of 1850. In retrospect, the wisdom of this strategy can hardly be doubted. If the South had chosen to secede in 1850, she almost surely would have succeeded, probably without a war (although that would have come later because the Ohio River could not be subject to two sovereignties). The ensuing decade saw the North badly outstrip the South in growth of population and industrial power. The Midwest, traditionally oriented toward New Orleans, came to trade through New York City. Ten years witnessed a profound shift in the balance of power.

Horace Greeley prided himself as the champion of the common man. Part of his pose was to avoid the snobbishness of using his private carriage for travel to and from his office; each morning he would board the horse-drawn streetcar on Broadway. If a seat on the wide "democratic" rear bench was available, he took it. One day the docker seated beside him was reading Charles A. Dana's *New York Sun.*

Greeley: "Why do you read the *Sun,* friend? Why not the *Tribune?"*

Longshoreman: "The *Tribune?* I only use that to wipe me arse with."

Greeley: "Keep it up, friend, keep it up. You'll soon have more sense in your ass than you've got now in your head."

ITS RELEVANCE

Greeley, born 1811, grew up concurrently with the mass-circulation urban newspaper. On the eve of the Civil War, his *New York Tribune* probably had more influence in the North and West than any other daily. He used it to proclaim a wide spectrum of reforms: the utopian socialism called Fourierism imported from France, temperance, women's rights, a homestead law, abolition of slavery. But we must suspect that these aberrant causes harmed his circulation.

What his paper offered was a lively account of recent events. Further, Greeley, like his contemporary President Lincoln, had a wit that was telling but not delicate. The United States from 1830 to 1860 made few claims to gentility. Those would come after the War.

Senator Orville H. Platt was back home in Connecticut in 1894. One day he was out in his buggy seeking to mend his political fences among his constituents. As he drove along a country road he spotted a farmer standing in his field near the fence. Platt drew up his horse and clambered down onto the roadside. As the two men exchanged laconic "Good mornings," a herd of sheep came along a cross road.

Farmer: "Them sheep been shorn."

Platt: " 'Pears so, at least on this side."

ITS RELEVANCE

Platt, along with Nelson W. Aldrich of Rhode Island, William B. Allison of Iowa, and John C. Spooner of Wisconsin, formed a quadrumvirate who—by reason of intellectual force, parliamentary skill, and seniority—dominated the United States Senate for three decades at the turn of the century. Aldrich virtually dictated the high-tariff acts. Platt specialized in refuting all arguments that favored an effective anti-trust policy. The others rounded up votes from the agricultural Midwest for bills that were antagonistic to the interests of the agricultural Midwest.

The caution of American politicians, their penchant for shunning all commitments and hedging all bets, is proverbial. One ancient saw goes like this: "If you want to know what a politician is up to, don't watch his mouth, watch his feet." They are hard men to back into corners. The tactic is necessary for survival.

ANECDOTE

At the beginning of the twentieth century when Carter Harrison was mayor of Chicago, his mouthpiece in the city council was Little Mike Ryan. Michael was notorious for hiking every appropriations bill, confident that it was a "job" and that he would get his rake-off. So his peers were astounded when he rose one day in opposition to a proposal to buy six gondolas for the lagoon in Lincoln Park. Little Mike was on an economy drive.

"Why waste the taxpayers' money buying six gondolas? Git a pair of 'em and let nature take its course."

ITS RELEVANCE

In many times and places, Americans have loved to denigrate the faculties—moral and intellectual—of their elected leaders. Politicians are both fools and crooks, is the accepted byword. When it becomes clear that George Norris and George McGovern are not knaves, the defense mechanism is to conclude that they must be stupid.

Conversely, a few of the bolder politicians can take potshots at the society that they are supposed to govern. The black man Carl Stokes, during the short span when he presided over Cleveland, announced: "I'm mayor of the only city in the world with a river that's a fire hazard." Those who have seen the Cuyahoga River will know that Stokes was not just joking; it has caught fire.

The superintendent of schools in Pontotoc County, Mississippi was compaigning for re-election. His opponent was, for those parts, a well-to-do farmer who had attended the University of Georgia. Speaking to a crowd of rednecks:

Incumbent: "That other fellow was so uppity that he went to college. Worse than that, we got a fine university right here in our own proud state; reckon some of you folks been to Oxford over in the next county and seen it. Worst of all, wait until you hear what they do at that fancy school in Athens.

"Lots of truthful folks have told me that the superintendent there—never git to be superintendent around here—he lets the boys and girls matriculate together. Why, they even use the same curriculum. And after years of sin and shame, the boys and girls go to vespers together. The wind-up of all this corruption is that they share the baccalaureate.

"Do you good people want a man who spent a misguided youth in a place like that to be the shepherd over your babies?"

ITS RELEVANCE

The absurdity of the story is obvious since no politician in northeastern Mississippi (however slanderous his purpose) would talk to an audience in a string of polysyllabic words with Latinate roots. But with jokes as with other libels: their falsity does not reduce their popularity. A good many city sophisticates delight in canards against the rubes from the boondocks. Just listening titillates them.

ANECDOTE

When Grover Cleveland, governor of New York, was the Democratic nominee for President in 1884, his opponents revealed that he was the father of an illegitimate child. Cleveland admitted the charge, but won the election by a narrow margin. Democratic rowdies produced this chant:

Hurray for Maria,
Hurray for the kid,
We voted for Grover,
And damned glad we did.

ITS RELEVANCE

Although the historians' guild has had some muckrakers, most American scholars do not dwell on the deviances of our public men. To cite another instance, President Warren G. Harding has now been exposed by the discovery of his correspondence with his mistress; rumors had it that he, before entering the White House in 1921, had engaged in intimate relations with her in the anteroom to the Senate Chamber of the United States. It is reported that Harding, in his adulthood, was told by his father: "Warren, it's a lucky thing you weren't born a girl; you'd always be in a family way."

But *Notable American Women* (3 vols., 1971), while including dozens of poetasters, obscure opera singers, and such like, expunges both of these women from the record. Weren't they notable? How many women have been mistress to a future President? And caught at it. What ever happened in this set to Maria Reynolds, the mistress of Alexander Hamilton, a Founding Father? We need not trouble over the paramours of Gouverneur Morris, another Founding Father. They were too numerous to list—but Morris did keep a statistical tally of the hundreds with whom he had shared a bed, or a carriage, or a floor in the private dining room of an inn, or wherever.

Just before the state of New York extended the franchise to women (1917), a band of suffragettes staged a parade on Fifth Avenue. The police broke it up and hauled off dozens of demonstrators in their paddy wagons. A veteran of the war for women's rights was thrust into a cell with a neophyte, who was in tears thinking of the disgrace that her arrest would bring to her family. At last the veteran could stand the commotion no longer.

Young woman: "Oh, what will I do? What'll I say?"

Veteran: "Don't worry, dear, trust in God. She will watch over you."

ITS RELEVANCE

God keeps changing both sex and color as militant movements for equal rights wax and wane. In the 1960's, Harlem stores were selling crucifixes that portrayed a black Christ.

Two aspects of the campaign for woman suffrage may be noted. On a statewide basis, it first succeeded where women were scarce: Wyoming in 1890, Colorado in 1893, Utah in 1896. In other states a restricted suffrage was already being granted to women in contests where they were thought to have a special concern (such as school boards).

During World War I, the editors of a radical magazine—cartoonist Art Young, John Reed immortalized by his reportage of the Russian Revolution in *Ten Days That Shook the World* (1919), and author Max Eastman—were indicted under the Sedition Act for obstructing the war effort. On toward the conclusion of their trial, the prosecutor in his summation to the jury became eloquent about his nephew who had been killed in France, but Art Young was sleeping through the rhetoric.

Prosecutor: "He died for John Reed, he died for Max Eastman . . ."

Young (waking up): "Didn't he die for me?"

Reed (patting Young on his bald head): "Never mind, Art, Jesus died for you."

ITS RELEVANCE

All we can say for sure is that American radicalism lost its sense of humor and its following at the same time. As to causal relations between the two phenomena, others must judge. In regard to wit, the *Daily Worker* could not play in the same league with the old *Masses.*

Calvin Coolidge as governor of Massachusetts was asked whether he had taken part in college sports. "Yes, I held the stakes."

Coolidge as President one day was out meandering with a Senator. As they came up to the White House on their return, the Senator said flippantly: "I wonder who lives there."

Coolidge: "Nobody. They just come and go."

Alice Roosevelt Longworth (daughter of Theodore Roosevelt) said that Coolidge looked like he'd been weaned on a pickle.

When President Theodore Roosevelt was in Cambridge, Massachusetts, he stayed at the official mansion of Charles William Eliot, top dog at Harvard. A reporter called there to interview Roosevelt.

Reporter: "I want to see the President."

Maid: "Oh, not now sir. He's busy with Mr. Roosevelt."

Senator, later President, John F. Kennedy wrote this one down. You could clear the room at any meeting of the Board of Aldermen in Chicago about 1900 by bursting into the room and shouting:

"Alderman—your saloon is on fire."

THEIR RELEVANCE

Kennedy should have known; he belonged to the third generation of a tribe of glittering politicians. (The first generation is represented mainly by his maternal grandfather, Honey Jim Fitzgerald, boss of Boston.)

As these examples suggest, Presidential humor since Lincoln has tended to be constricted to the one-liner.

ANECDOTE

President John F. Kennedy sent his brother, Attorney General Robert F. Kennedy, to Massachusetts to buy a burial plot. When Bobby got back to Washington he was ecstatic about the location in the foothills near Williamstown.

RFK: "Its beauty is incredible. Twenty acres. And it only costs $50,000."

JFK: "Only $50,000, the fool says. I'll only be there three days."

ITS RELEVANCE

The myth don't speak ill of the dead is persistent. After President Kennedy was assassinated, nobody was telling jokes like this for several years. But then, Kennedy was a myth in himself. Never before had such a mediocre President gained so much renown.

As long as a Chief Executive is alive, folks think that any slander is fair. Kennedy's successor (and his assassin) were greeted with graffito as: "Lee Harvey Oswald, where are you now when your country really needs you?"

"What is an administrator?"

"A man who reaches his desk promptly at 9 each morning. In the middle of the desk he finds a molehill. By the time he leaves promptly at 5, he has built a mountain."

ITS RELEVANCE

My friend Ramsay Macmullen of Yale, a specialist in the late Roman Empire, has brilliantly argued on the basis of his monographic work that perhaps every large bureaucracy by its nature must produce directives and orders and memos that use endless battalions of multisyllable words to say nothing. After trying without hope to fend off the flood of paper, nearly all of it telling me what I already knew or what I didn't need to know, I commented facetiously that only a province-wide forest fire in British Columbia could save us. Here are some choice items of gobbledegook from recent Washington:

Army sent around a memo that AR 380-40 is now amended so that all references to KAG - 1 / TSEC and KAG - 2 / TSEC will now read KAG - 1A / TSEC and KAG - 2A / TSEC.

Navy beat. Upon protest about the number of missives flying around, they circulated a new form: QUESTIONNAIRE ON FREQUENCY OF UNNECESSARY FORMS.

Navy operates its own messhall in the White House. An order decreed that the label "White House Mess" should be removed from its matchbook covers.

ANECDOTE

In 1963 a contingent from the State Department journeyed to South America for a conference of the Organization of American States, where the United States hoped to achieve unanimity among the member nations for a condemnation of the government of Cuba. When the Americans returned to Washington, one junketeer submitted a supplementary expense account:

taxicabs $14.30
lunch with Guatemalan delegation $6,000,000

ITS RELEVANCE

By such wily stratagems are diplomatic victories scored. If you can't persuade 'em, buy 'em.

In the years after the Castro regime came to power in Cuba in 1959, the efforts of the American government to topple it ranged from vulgarity to violence. Some Americans retaliated against their own leaders by making up yarns such as this one. How much truth was contained in these canards? Probably quite a bit, but even our grandchildren may not know for sure.

Historians, notoriously an earnest bunch, do not pay much attention to humor. Americans in general like to tell jokes but do not bother to theorize about them. Probably this trait is largely to the good. But the impression persists, even though it is seldom scrutinized, that Americans laugh when Englishmen would not, and vice versa. For myself, I have never been able to manage even a chuckle when reading books by Stephen Potter.

A precious band of our countrymen have asked in various ways: What is peculiar about our native anecdotes that causes us to be amused? Constance Rourke's pioneering *American Humor: A Study of the National Character* (1931) is not a collection of tales and skits but an analysis of them. After delineating the stock funny men—Yankee, backwoodsman, Negro minstrel—she focuses on "that perpetual travel which often seemed the single enduring feature of the country." The mobility of Americans (geographic, personal, social, family) ensured that nobody would be in face-to-face contact with another individual for more than an instant. The essence of existence was to make a quick and striking impression, sign up the order as it were, and swiftly move along. Migrants learned to exaggerate: If British humor is understated, American specializes in hyperbole. For the same reason, the wanderers learned to shift their character to counter new circumstances, often badly perceived. The American reached into his grab bag and emerged wearing a different mask. Perhaps the national character meant to have no fixed individuality, no set pattern of values and reflexes. "It pays to be shifty in a new country."

Walter Blair's *Native American Humor (1800–1900)* (1937) is both a collection of examples and an appraisal. It deals almost solely with written tales, which form only a small part of the whole. Like Rourke, he can find little that was "native" to American wit until about 1840 (nor was there much that was witty in the jest books of the eighteenth century). After giving his definition of "American humor," Blair organizes his illustrations entirely in terms of subcategories. Significantly, except for a great artist like Mark Twain, his species are entirely regional: Down East, Old Southwest, and so on.

In *The Charming Idioms of New England* (1960), Arthur H. Cole made a virtue of parochialism. He is concerned to taste the spices of simile and metaphor with which Yankees flavored their speech around 1900. His specimens were oral, not written. To this mundane material of the common folk he brings the same depth of interpretation that distinguishes his work in economic history. He regrets, politely as is his wont, "the general lack of attention by scholars to this range of inquiry." One conclusion is: "the utilization of a complex sophisticated collection of similes and metaphors, shared with his friends in the New England world, gave the individual inhabitant a sense of belonging . . ."

This viewpoint suits me—up to a point. We like to laugh with our friends, sure. But only with our friends. We like to laugh AT those who differ from us. Reading through the above pages, I am struck by the frequency of American jokes that stem from dislike or even malice. Many of the Polack jokes seem to me very funny, but only when I fail to take the sensitivities of Polish Americans into account. Some of the sex jokes make you laugh if you can forget that women are human beings. And so on. Judging from the perspective of American humor, the "consensus" interpretation of our history has been wrong all the time. Americans have always disliked the outsiders. If jokes serve to bind together the in-group, and they do, they violently repel those who are seen as a threat to the traditional code. Whether the humor of other nations has a similar quality, somebody else must say.

139 Ray Ginger was born in Tennessee in 1924. Reared there and in Indiana, he was further educated at three universities in the Midwest. He has taught at Case-Western Reserve, Harvard, Brandeis, Wayne State, and in summer sessions at Stanford and Sir George Williams. In 1966 he was director of the Telluride Association Summer Field Program at Hampton, Virginia. Presently professor of history at the University of Calgary in Alberta, Canada, he lives in a modest coal-mining village in the Rockies. He swears that all the money in Christendom would not lure him back to a metropolis again.